NEEDLEPOINT GIFTS
For All Seasons

NEEDLEPOINT GIFTS
For All Seasons

JUDY CLAYTON & DEBORAH DOW

David & Charles

Page 2 *The Spring Garden (page 43),*
Summer Garden (page 65),
Autumn Garden (page 95) and Winter Garden
(page 122) mounted together in one frame.

A DAVID & CHARLES BOOK

First published in the UK in 1996

Text and designs Copyright © Judy Clayton and Deborah Dow 1996
Photography and layout Copyright © David & Charles 1996

Judy Clayton and Deborah Dow have asserted their right to be identified as authors of this work
in accordance with the Copyright, Designs and Patents Act, 1988.

A catalogue record for this book is available from the British Library.

ISBN 0 7153 0317 1

Photography by Di Lewis
Book design by Anita Ruddell
Printed in Great Britain
by Butler & Tanner Ltd Frome
for David & Charles
Brunel House   Newton Abbot Devon

CONTENTS

INTRODUCTION

*E*ach season unfolds with the promise of many special occasions to come in the forthcoming months. With these in mind, and our love of needlepoint, we were inspired to compile the projects for *Needlepoint Gifts for all Seasons*.

In this book you will find ideas to appeal to all ages – from the tiny tooth fairy pillow to the crinolined lady spectacle case. Although you could mount nearly all of the designs as pictures, many of the projects also have a very practical nature. This may be welcome news to avid needleworkers who usually have too little wall space left to display their handiwork. Needlepoint pincushions and needlecases, a jewellery roll and trinket box lids are among some of the decorative but also functional gifts. In each season there are individual designs which have a common theme which can be made up into one large design, along with small greetings cards quickly completed for that treasured day.

Although many of the designs are quite small, they are full of the colours and feelings reflected by each of the four seasons. They are all stitched on canvas using stranded cottons (floss), principally because there is such a wonderful colour palette to choose from, but also because cotton is lovely to work with at any time of the year. To add extra depth and detail, metallic threads and coloured glass beads have been applied to some of the designs.

Simple tent stitch is used for most of the projects but other stitches have also been incorporated to create more diversity and texture. The Basic Techniques chapter at the beginning of the book gives a step-by-step guide to all the stitches as well as general information on materials and ideas for finishing the projects. The less confident stitcher will find projects with fewer colours or larger areas of one colour easier to start with, whereas designs like the Hollyhocks picture (see page 50) use several different stitches and are a little more demanding. The Autumn patchwork cushion, with its squares of different stitches, makes an excellent introduction to the stitches used throughout the book.

Each design has been beautifully photographed and has an easy to follow full-colour chart. Several of the designs show alternative colourways and the various alphabets featured can always be used to personalise an individual piece.

The projects in this book follow the tradition of Thumbelina Designs, the needlework kit business that we started ten years ago. If you would like further information on these kits then please write to Thumbelina Designs, 10 Barley Mow Passage, London W4 4PH.

We hope this book gives you many happy hours of stitching.

Opposite: *The seasonal fruit tile pictures: Crabapple Tile (top left), Cherries Tile (top right), Blackberries Tile (bottom left), Cranberries Tile (bottom right).*

BASIC TECHNIQUES

In this section you will find all the information you need to begin to work all the projects in this book including advice on materials required, working stitches and finishing off the finished pieces.

MATERIALS AND EQUIPMENT

CANVAS

The projects in this book are worked on single interlocked canvas that has either 18 or 22 holes per inch (7 or 10 holes per centimetre). Always buy canvas from a well known manufacturer (a good needlework shop will advise you) as cheap canvas may have an uneven weave, knots or broken threads which will distort the finished piece. White canvas has been used throughout this book, as many of the designs use pastel colours.

Always leave a border of approximately 1½ in (4cm) around the design. To prevent the canvas fraying or catching your threads as you sew, seal the edges with masking tape.

NEEDLES

A number 22 tapestry needle is needed for most of the designs. It is the perfect size for 18 hole canvas as it will not fall straight through the canvas threads, nor is it big enough to push the threads apart and distort the weave. Where a different size needle is required it will be stated in the list of materials for that particular design.

Steel needles may eventually snag, rust or bend after a lot of use, and will catch on the canvas, so have spare needles available. Gold plated needles have a much longer life and will not rust.

You will need a beading needle for any design that incorporates beads. These needles are very thin and pliable in order to get through the small holes in the beads.

THREADS

Most of the projects in this book use stranded cotton (floss), which is readily available in hundreds of colours from good needlework shops. DMC and Anchor threads are most commonly available. We list colours from both for each design, and although DMC and Anchor colours are not exactly the same, the shades indicated are as close a match as possible.

You will need one skein of each colour unless otherwise specified in the materials list for a particular design. Each skein is approximately 8¾ yards (8 metres) long and is made up of a thread that can be divided into six separate strands. Most of the projects use a combination of three strands. Where four or more are used (or sometimes fewer) this will be stated in the individual instructions for each design (see under Stitching below). Other threads used include metallic threads for added sparkle, perlé which is a rope–like thread that cannot be split, and English Flower Threads.

Use a thread length of 15in (37cm) for the stranded cottons (floss), perlé and Flower Threads, and a shorter length of 10in (25cm) for metallic threads, which are prone to split. Do not attempt to save time by using longer lengths as they will only knot or tangle.

OTHER MATERIALS

□ Scissors – a medium sized pair for cutting and trimming canvas and a small pair with pointed ends for cutting threads.
□ Masking tape to bind canvas edges.
□ Graph paper for charting letters or names.

GETTING STARTED

The designs in this book are small enough to be worked in your hand and therefore do not require a frame, unless you find using one more comfortable.

Choose a good light in which to work. If you can't work in daylight, try using a daylight bulb which simulates natural light. Magnifying glasses and lamps specifically for needleworkers are also commonly available.

Do keep your hands and working area clean as light threads will show any dirt.

CENTERING THE DESIGN ON THE CANVAS
To make sure your design fits well on your piece of canvas you must always start working from the centre point. Fold the canvas in half and half again to find the centre, and mark this point with a pencil or marker. Find the centre point on the chart by counting the number of stitches along a vertical and horizontal side and dividing by two.

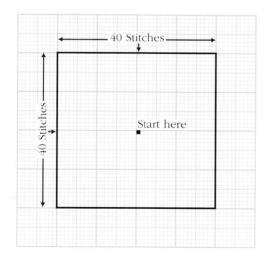

How to find a centre point

STITCHING
Firstly, separate the thread into six strands and recombine three or more strands as specified. This will help prevent the thread twisting.

Cut lengths of threads approximately 15 inches/40cm long for working details and motifs, and 20 inches/50cm for large areas of background colour. Do not be tempted to use longer lengths as they will tangle and knot.

Sometimes strands of different colours are combined to give a shaded effect and this will be noted in the colour code on the chart.

Work in blocks of colour from the central point or where specified in the instructions for your chosen design. A starting point is suggested for each design, which may be a prominent motif or a borderline. Count the number of stitches the starting point is from the centre point and mark it on the canvas, so you know where to begin.

Begin each block of colour by pushing the needle up through the canvas. Holding the end of the thread underneath, sew over it with your first few stitches. Do not knot the ends as they will leave bumps under the finished work.

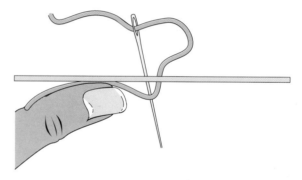

Starting

If two areas of the same colour are close together you may jump across a few stitches; otherwise finish off the thread by running it through a worked row on the reverse of the piece and cut it off neatly.

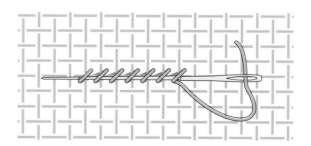

Finishing

THE STITCHES

The stitches used in this book are described on the following pages. Follow the numbers on the accompanying diagrams to help you form each stitch. Always bring the needle up through hole number 1 from the reverse of the fabric, and down through hole number 2 and so on. With many of the stitches you will need filling stitches to complete the design. Simply work as much of the pattern as possible and then fill in the remaining gaps with smaller stitches.

Detail from the Autumn Patchwork Cushion (page 86): the perfect opportunity to try out most of the stitches featured in this book on a single project

Diagonal Mosaic	Leaf	Double Cross	Byzantine
Cushion			Eyelet
Rice			Broad Cross
Rhodes	Moorish	Milanese	Large Cross

TENT STITCH

Tent stitch is the basic needlepoint stitch and is used in most of the designs in this book. It is a simple diagonal stitch over one thread of canvas. It can be worked vertically or horizontally, from right to left or left to right, or from top to bottom or bottom to top. However, you must always make sure that there is a long diagonal stitch on the reverse of your work, otherwise the stitching will appear rather thin from the front. If used for large areas of stitching, tent stitch has a tendency to distort the canvas, so it is better to use basketweave stitch (see page 14).

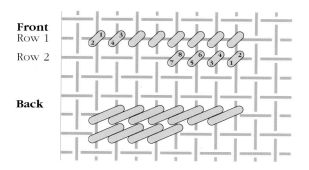

Tent stitch

CUSHION STITCH

Made up of diagonal stitches, beginning with a stitch going over one thread, followed by further diagonal stitches going over increasing numbers of threads, ie, one, two, three, four and then back down to one, making a complete square.

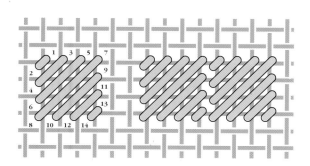

Cushion stitch

SLOPING GOBELIN STITCH

Work diagonal stitch like tent stitch but over two canvas threads.

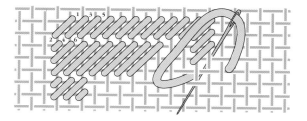

Sloping gobelin stitch

LONG STITCH OR SATIN STITCH

Long stitch is made up of straight stitches going vertically or horizontally over a certain number of canvas threads. It can be worked in straight rows over the same number of threads, randomly over differing numbers of threads, or in a pattern creating perhaps a row of triangles or diamond shapes.

Satin stitch is a long stitch worked diagonally over the canvas threads and is useful for making leaf shapes or border patterns.

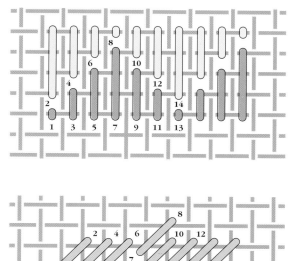

Long stitch or satin stitch

CROSS STITCH AND LARGE CROSS STITCH

To work cross stitches on canvas it is best to stitch the area in tent stitch first and then go back over them with tent stitches following the opposite diagonal. This gives good coverage at the back. Traditional cross stitch does not give such good coverage, and the stitching can seem thin on canvas. Large cross stitches are worked over two intersections of canvas.

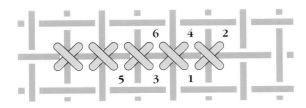

Cross stitch

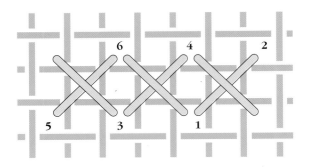

Large cross stitch

BYZANTINE STITCH

Similar to Jacquard stitch but made up of steps of sloping gobelin stitch alone.

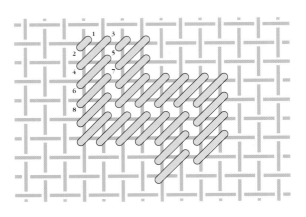

Byzantine stitch

FRENCH KNOTS

French knots are used decoratively to make flowers and accentuate small details. Bring the thread up through the square. Wrap the thread around the needle once (twice for a large knot) and pass the needle down into a hole adjacent to where the thread comes up. Pull the needle through carefully, allowing the thread to form a knot on the surface.

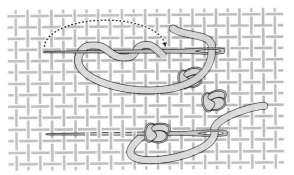

French knots

JACQUARD STITCH

Work steps of sloping gobelin stitch over two canvas threads sandwiched by tent stitches. The steps can be made up of any number of stitches but the amount must be the same in any one design. The tent stitches could be worked in a different colour to the sloping gobelin stitches.

Moorish stitch (see Autumn Patchwork Cushion, page 86) is a variation of Jacquard stitch where a diagonal stitch (see page 15) is bordered by rows of tent stitches.

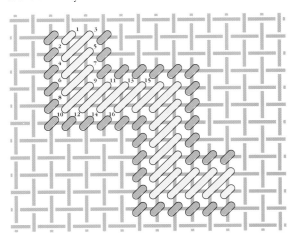

Jacquard stitch

MILANESE STITCH

This gives the effect of triangle shapes running diagonally across the canvas. Each run of triangles may be a different colour, creating a striking geometric pattern.

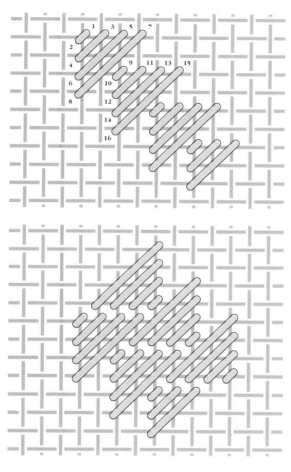

Milanese stitch

CHAIN STITCH

Chain stitches have been oversewn onto several designs as they make a good leaf shape. Come

Chain stitch

up in hole 1 make a loop of thread and go back down into hole 1. Then come up in hole 2, catch the loop and go back down into hole three.

LEAF STITCH

Straight stitches fan out from a central run of holes, and can be made different sizes by altering the length of the long stitches. Follow the numbers on the diagram as follows: 1–2, 3–4, 5–6, 7–8, 9–10, 11–10, 12–10, 13–8, 14–6, 15–4, 16–2. Neighbouring stitches are worked into holes already used, so that there are no gaps showing between stitches.

Leaf stitch

BACK STITCH

This is used to outline areas of colour using one strand of thread. Pass the needle up through square 1, down through square 2, up through square 3, and so on. You will have a double length stitch on the reverse side of the work. Backstitch can be worked in any direction. Complete all the tent stitch areas before working backstitch outlines.

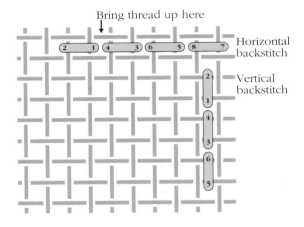

Back stitch

BRICK STITCH

Long stitches are worked horizontally or vertically over any number of threads, with the subsequent rows interlocking to give the effect of a brick wall.

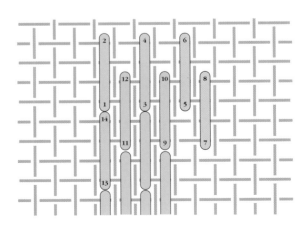

Brick stitch

BASKETWEAVE STITCH

Basketweave is a tent stitch that is worked diagonally across the canvas always starting in the top right hand corner of the design. It is generally used for background filling as it does not result in the canvas being distorted.

Front

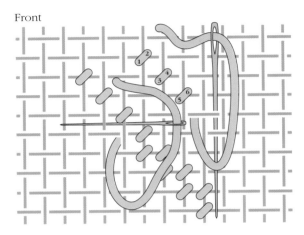

Back

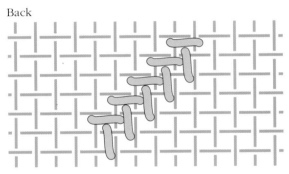

Basketweave stitch

FLOWER STITCH

Worked in a similar way to eyelet stitch but forming a circular or star shaped stitch rather than a square.

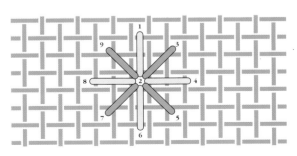

Flower stitch

RICE STITCH

Work a large cross stitch over four threads of canvas, followed by a diagonal stitch over each corner of the cross, starting at the centre of each side. These top stitches could be of a different colour to the base stitch.

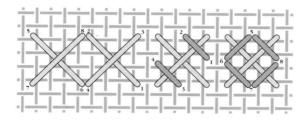

Rice stitch

DIAGONAL STITCH

This is made up of cushion stitches that run diagonally across the canvas. The corner stitch of each cushion is omitted so that a stepped effect is created.

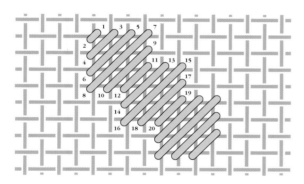

Diagonal stitch

DOUBLE CROSS STITCH

Work a straight cross stitch over four threads of canvas. Then oversew with a diagonal cross

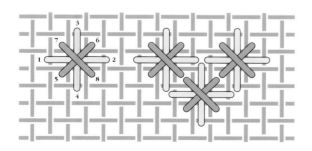

Double cross stitch

stitch over two threads, giving the effect of a star. The straight cross and diagonal cross can be worked in different colours which gives a more textured effect.

RHODES STITCH

A square stitch made by crossing the thread across the square like the spokes of a wheel. It can be worked over different numbers of threads to make it larger or smaller. Finish it off by working a small straight stitch over the threads at the centre of the square.

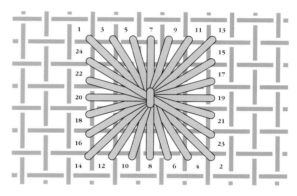

Rhodes stitch

FLORENTINE STITCH

Work long horizontal or vertical stitches of equal length in a zig–zag pattern. Alternate rows of colours can be stitched to give a dramatic effect.

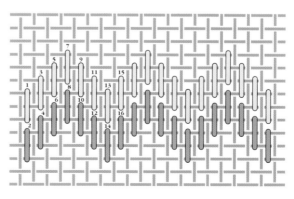

Florentine stitch

BROAD CROSS STITCH

Work the centre diagonal of a cushion stitch over four threads and the two stitches each side of it, then follow with a central diagonal worked in the opposite direction with the two stitches each side of that. These could be worked in different colours.

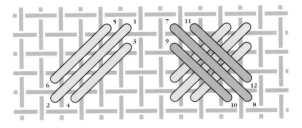

Broad cross stitch

DIAGONAL MOSAIC STITCH

Work alternate tent and sloping gobelin stitches diagonally across the canvas.

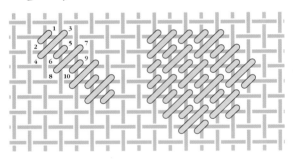

Diagonal mosaic stitch

EYELET STITCH

A square stitch worked by bringing the needle up at the edges of the square and down into the centre each time. On the diagram the centre stitch is number 2, so work 1–2, 3–2, 4–2, 5–2, etc.

Eyelet stitch

OVERSEWING

As the name suggests this stitch is worked after the design is finished and therefore creates a more three-dimensional effect. Most of the oversewing in this book is done using one strand of thread and a long stitch to make whiskers or fences or to outline certain parts of the design.

FOLLOWING THE CHARTS AND FINISHING

THE CHART AND COLOUR KEY

The charts are not actual size, so it is not possible to place the canvas on top of the chart and trace the design through.

Each coloured or blank square on the chart generally indicates one stitch, i.e., one intersection of canvas. Different symbols are used if there are several shades of a certain colour.

The colour code on the chart gives the DMC colour numbers. The closest Anchor equivalent can be found on the colour and stitch key. Other threads required are listed in the colour key for each design.

Alongside the colour key is a stitch key, stating which stitch should be used for that particular colour. If the number of combined threads varies it will also be noted here.

Measurements for the finished projects and canvas size are all approximate.

GRAPHING LETTERS AND NUMBERS

A number of the projects incorporate a name, date or initials to commemorate an event or personalise the design. There are alphabet charts throughout the book from which you may draw out your particular details onto a sheet of graph paper. First, mark the space allotted for the letters on to the graph paper then pencil in your name etc, leaving one space between each letter or three spaces between each initial. To centre your name, make sure you have an even number of blank stitches each side of the lettering.

You may find it easier to draw your name on graph paper, count the number of stitches it uses (including spaces) and deduct this from the number of stitches available in the space of the design. Divide the result by two to get the number of blank stitches you need on each side of the lettering to place the name centrally.

BLOCKING AND STRETCHING

When your needlepoint is complete it may need stretching to get it back into shape. This is called blocking. You will need a clean, smooth, thick board large enough to hold the finished needlepoint, a sheet of card, blotting paper, tacks and pins, and a piece of cloth.

Make a template of the outline of the design on the card, and pin to the board. Place the needlepoint face down on to the template and secure one corner with a pin. Cover with the damp cloth, use a steam iron to gently press the needlepoint and carefully pull the three

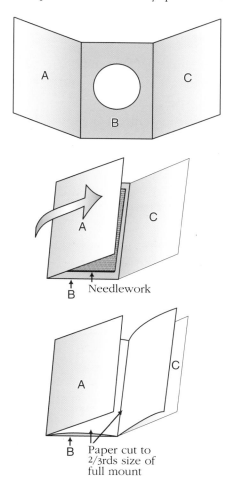

Mounting your needlework in a three-fold mount card

remaining corners out to fit the template. Pin them down, and softly press with the iron, barely touching the work. Leave to dry for a few hours before removing from the board.

MOUNTING CARDS

The greetings cards and bookmarks in this book have been mounted in three–fold card mounts, widely available in needlework or craft shops or by mail order.

To mount your finished and blocked work, trim the edge to ⅜in (1cm). Fit it into the aperture in section B of the card mount and stick it down using craft glue (PVA), spray mount or double sided tape. Place the needlework right side down on the table and fold section A over section B. Before gluing section A in place you can insert a slip of paper to write a message on between the needlepoint and section A of the card. If using dark mount cards, slip a piece of white paper behind the needlework to prevent shadowing.

FRAMING

To frame your completed needlework you can either buy a ready–made frame or have one made by a professional picture framer. If you find a ready–made or second hand frame, allow a mount border of approximately 1½ to 2in (4 to 5cm) around the design. A professional will be able to cut a mount to fit and should also be able to supply a backing board, cord and hook. Whether you choose to have a frame specially made or use a ready–made frame, take time to research all the different types of mouldings and colours of mount board as both can enhance the final appearance of your work.

Glass may be used to protect the needlepoint but should not touch the stitching, so a double mount or spacers must be used. The glass may obscure the texture of the stitching.

MAKING UP PROJECTS

Instructions and diagrams for making up designs into cushions, picture or photograph frames, bows, buttons, pincushions, box lids and needle or spectacle cases are given with each individual project.

SPRING

When daisies pied and violets blue
And ladysmocks all silver white
And cuckoo buds of yellow hue
Do paint the meadows with delight
WILLIAM SHAKESPEARE

Spring – the countryside and garden begin to awaken from the cold days of winter. It is the season of new beginnings, fresh green growth, delicate blossoms, pale skies and dewy mornings. Daffodils and crocuses colour woodlands and gardens, followed by the rich blue carpets of bluebells. Pastel shades of pinks, blues, pale yellows and soft greens are used together in these springtime designs, with a mixture of simple needlepoint stitches, to create texture and pattern. There are floral projects for special occasions – Easter, Mother's Day, moving house, or the birth of a new baby; and delightful designs such as the chequered mirror frames, or the duck and rabbit egg cosies which make ideal Easter gifts for adults and children.

New Baby Card

In delicate shades of pink, blue and yellow this dainty little card with its shy little rabbit, makes a lovely keepsake for a new baby

DESIGN SIZE 3⅛ x 3¼ (7.9 x 8.2cm)
STITCHES Tent stitch, cushion stitch, long stitch, rhodes stitch, sloping gobelin stitch

□ Needle, size 22
□ Canvas 18 holes per inch (7 holes per

centimetre), 6 x 6in (15 x 15cm)

□ Stranded cottons (floss) as listed on chart key. Use three strands of thread unless stated otherwise
□ Card mount, three-fold with pre-cut 3⅛ x 3¼ in (7.9 x 8.2cm) aperture

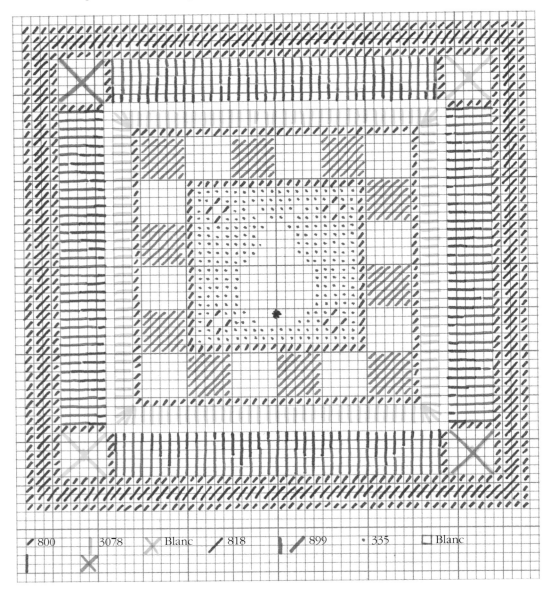

| / 800 | 3078 | ✕ Blanc | / 818 | 899 | • 335 | □ Blanc |

New Baby Card and Tooth Fairy Pillow (page 22).

1 Find and mark the centre point on the canvas (see page 9).

2 Count from the centre point to the inner blue square border and start stitching here. Complete the inner square and work outwards, band by band. Using one strand of white, oversew the rabbit's whiskers. Using three strands of sky blue, make the rabbit's tail by working one French knot.

3 Block your needlepoint (see page 17).

4 Make up the card by following the instructions on page 17.

DMC	COLOUR	ANCHOR	STITCH	STRANDS
Blanc	White	01	Cushion	4
			Rhodes	3
800	Sky blue	120	Tent	3
			Long	4
335	Pink	38	Cushion	4
			Long	4
			Tent	3
899	Mid pink	25	Cushion	4
			Long	4
			Tent	3
818	Very pale pink	271	Sloping gobelin	4
3078	Lemon	292	Long	4
			Rhodes	3

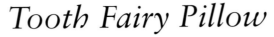

Tooth Fairy Pillow

Children will love to see if the tooth fairy has left them a coin in this tiny pillow. Destined to become part of the magic of childhood, it will be truly treasured

DESIGN SIZE 3½ x 3½ in (8.9 x 8.9cm)
STITCHES Tent stitch

☐ Needle, size 22
☐ Canvas 18 holes per inch (7 holes per centimetre), 6½ x 11½ in (16 x 30cm)
☐ Stranded cottons (floss) as listed on chart key. Use three strands of thread
☐ Backing fabric (cotton), white, 6½ x 11½ in (16 x 30cm)
☐ Kapok
☐ Blue ribbon, ⅜in x 12in (1cm x 30cm)

1 Find and mark the centre point on the canvas (see page 9).

2 Count from the centre point to the top right-hand corner of the outer blue border and start stitching here. Work both borders.

3 Using the alphabet on page 126, and following the instructions on page 16, stitch the child's name. This could be worked in dark blue if preferred. Work the rest of the design colour by colour including the separate fairy pocket.

4 Block your needlepoint (see page 17).

5 Cut the canvas surrounding the fairy pocket to ½ in (1cm) all round. Cut a square the same size as the pocket from the backing fabric. Place the needlepoint and the backing fabric right sides together. Using a suitably coloured thread, backstitch around three sides of the needlepoint as close to the edge of the stitching as possible. Trim the canvas to ¼ in (5mm) from the edge of the stitching and cut across the corners. Turn the right way out and press gently. Tuck under the remaining raw edges and sew up.

6 With the wrong side of the pocket and the right side of the pillow together, neatly stitch the pocket down around the blue border leaving the top open.

7 Repeat step 5 with the base of the pillow and the rest of the backing fabric, filling with kapok. Stitch the ribbon to the top of the pillow.

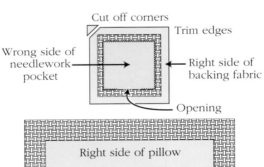

Making up the pillow

DMC	COLOUR	ANCHOR
793	Blue	176
800	Pale blue	120
335	Dark pink	38
899	Pink	25
818	Pale pink	271
700	Bright green	228
954	Pale green	203
743	Yellow	302
950	Flesh pink	1012
3778	Dark flesh	9575
Blanc	White	01

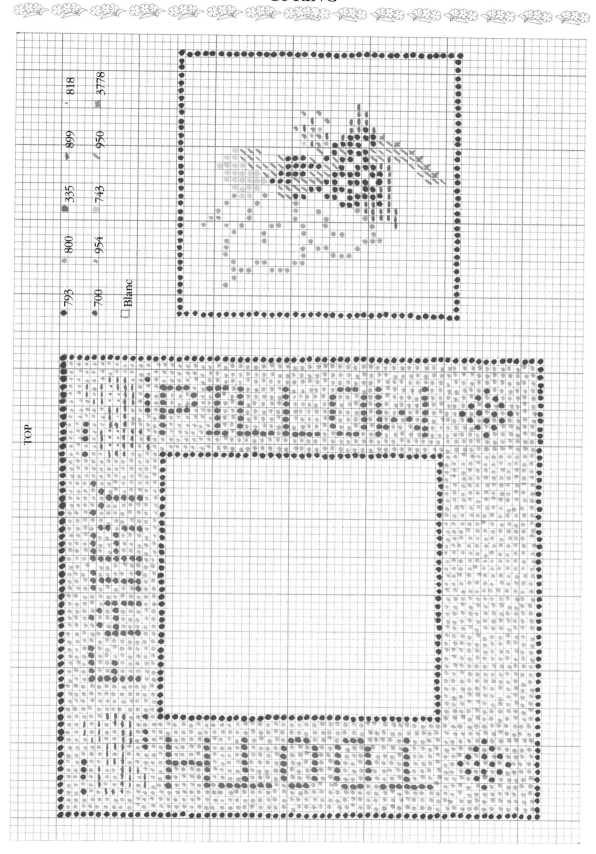

Wisteria Doorway Card

This beaded scene (shown on pages 18–19) makes an ideal moving house card

DESIGN SIZE 2½in (6.4cm) diameter
STITCHES Tent stitch

- Needle, size 22
- Beading needle
- Canvas 18 holes per inch (7 holes per centimetre), 4½ x 4½in (11.5 x 11.5cm)
- Stranded cotton (floss) as listed on chart key. Use three strands of thread unless stated otherwise
- Tiny glass seed beads in pearlised lilac
- Dark green card mount, three-fold with pre cut 2½in (6.4cm) round aperture

1 Find and mark the centre point on the canvas (see page 9).
2 Count the number of stitches from the centre point to the bottom right-hand corner of the doorway and start stitching here. Work colour by colour leaving the background until last.
3 Using one strand of black, outline the doorway, door panels and windows in backstitch.

Using one strand of white, create the window panes by oversewing in a criss-cross fashion.
4 Block your needlepoint (see page 17).
5 Using one strand of lilac and the beading needle, sew on the beads in a random fashion over the wisteria.
6 Make up the card by following the instructions on page 17.

DMC	COLOUR	ANCHOR
745	Cream	300
209	Lilac	109
211	Pale lilac	342
335	Dark pink	38
899	Pink	25
3326	Pale pink	24
3347	Green	261
471	Light green	255
310	Black	403
317	Dark grey	400
415	Light grey	398
841	Pale brown	379
Blanc	White	01

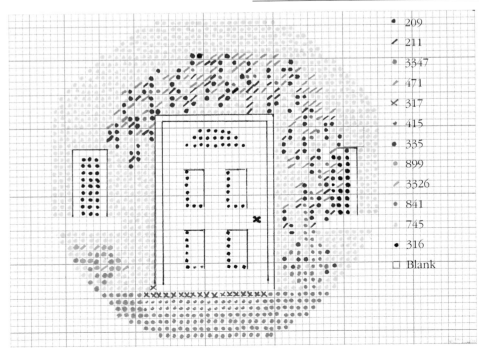

- 209
- 211
- 3347
- 471
- 317
- 415
- 335
- 899
- 3326
- 841
- 745
- 316
- Blank

Mother's Day Card

This pretty card reflects the pattern of an Elizabethan knot garden, with low box hedging and formal flower beds filled with springtime polyanthus

DESIGN SIZE 3⅛ x 3¼ in (7.9 x 8.2cm)
STITCHES Tent stitch, cross stitch, broad cross stitch, double cross stitch, long stitch sloping gobelin stitch

- ☐ Needle, size 22
- ☐ Canvas 18 holes per inch (7 holes per centimetre), 6 x 6in (15 x 15cm)
- ☐ Stranded cottons (floss) as listed on chart key. Use three strands of thread
- ☐ Card mount, three-fold with pre-cut 3⅛ in x 3¼ in (7.9 x 8.2cm) aperture.

DMC	Colour	Anchor
746	Cream	386
3348	Light green	264
3347	Green	261
351	Peach	10
353	Pale peach	8
793	Pale blue	176
791	Blue	178
209	Pale lilac	90
208	Lilac	99
335	Pink	38
349	Dark peach	13
744	Yellow	295

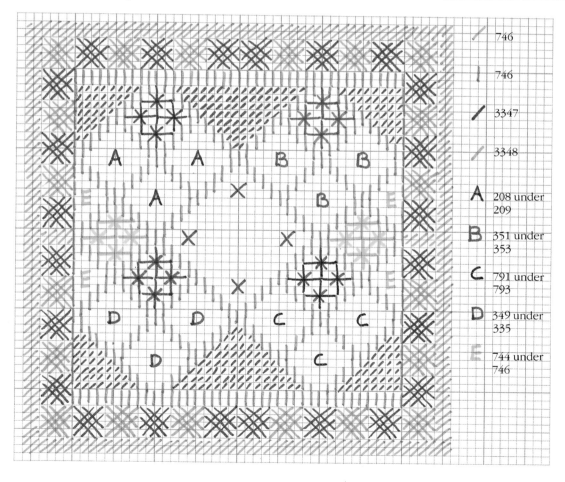

1 Find and mark the centre point on the canvas (see page 9).

2 Count from the centre point to the bottom right-hand corner of the inner square and work all the trellis pattern with lines of long stitch in cream over three horizontal threads of canvas.

3 Fill areas A, B, C, D, and E with four double cross stitches.

4 Using green and cross stitch, work the central initial 'M' for Mother or choose a letter from the alphabet on page 125. Work the four large cross stitches over two intersections of canvas. Work the background to the initial in cream in tent stitch.

5 Fill the remaining areas of the inner design with tent stitch in green.

6 Starting at each corner with light green, work a border of broad cross stitches, alternately in light green and green, around the inner border of the design. On the top and bottom rows two dark green stitches will meet in the centre. On the side rows there will be a gap which is filled with sloping gobelin stitch in light green.

7 Finally, work two borders of sloping gobelin stitch around the whole design in cream. Add more borders to make the design fit the aperture of your card if required.

8 Block your needlepoint (see page 17).

9 Make up the card by following the instructions on page 17. This design would also make a pretty scissor weight (see page 106).

Mother's Day Card and Monogrammed Brooch

Monogrammed Brooch

This delicate, personalised needlepoint brooch,
with a border of pink roses, is set in a simple, elegant, gilt frame
and makes a delightful present

DESIGN SIZE 1½ x 1⅛in (3.8 x 2.8cm)
STITCHES Tent stitch, French knots

□ Needle, size 24
□ Canvas 22 holes per inch (10 holes per centimetre), 4½ x 3½in (11.5 x 8.9cm)
□ Stranded cottons (floss) as listed on the chart key. Use three strands of thread unless stated otherwise
□ Gilt oval brooch frame, 1½ x 1⅛in (3.8 x 2.8cm)

1 Find and mark the centre point on the canvas (see page 9).
2 Count the number of stitches to the first dark pink stitch below the centre point and start stitching here. Work the floral border colour by colour.

3 Work an initial from the alphabet on page 125 by following the instructions on page 16, in the centre panel. Complete the background.
4 Using two strands of dark pink, work the French knots. Using two strands of green, over-sew the stems.
5 The gilt brooch frame is available from Framecraft. To mount, follow the makers instructions. You may need to trim the canvas very close to the stitches in order to fit the mount; and seal the edges with Fraycheck.

DMC	COLOUR	ANCHOR
309	Dark pink	39
335	Pink	38
3326	Pale pink	24
3347	Green	261
745	Cream	300
3348	Light green	264

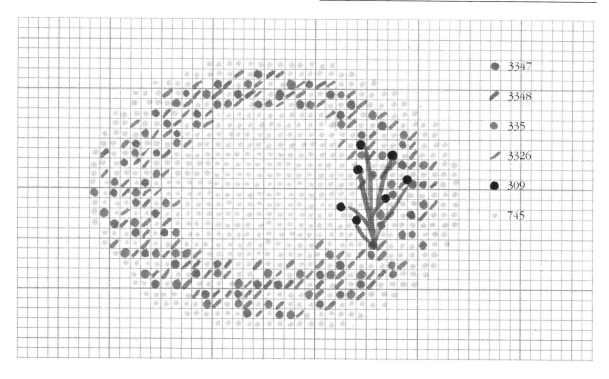

Easter Card

Easter eggs hidden in the long grass, a sunny daffodil, and the enduring symbol of Easter – the Cross (pictured on page 30).

DESIGN SIZE 2¼ x 3in (5.7 x 7.5cm)
STITCHES Tent stitch

☐ Needle, size 22
☐ Canvas 18 holes per inch (7 holes per centimetre), 6 x 6in (15 x 15cm)
☐ Stranded cottons (floss) as listed on chart key. Use three strands of thread unless otherwise stated
☐ Card mount, three-fold with pre-cut 2¼ x 3in (5.7 x 7.5cm) aperture

1 Find and mark the centre point on the canvas (see page 9).
2 Count from the centre point to the top of the cross and start stitching here. Work colour by colour. Back stitch round the daffodil as indicated on the chart using two strands of gold thread.
3 Block your needlepoint (see page 17).
4 Make up the card by following the instructions on page 17.

DMC	COLOUR	ANCHOR
3348	Light green	264
3347	Green	261
772	Very light green	259
742	Gold	303
743	Yellow	302
744	Pale yellow	301
745	Cream	300
798	Blue	131
309	Rose	39
794	Light blue	939
Blanc	White	01

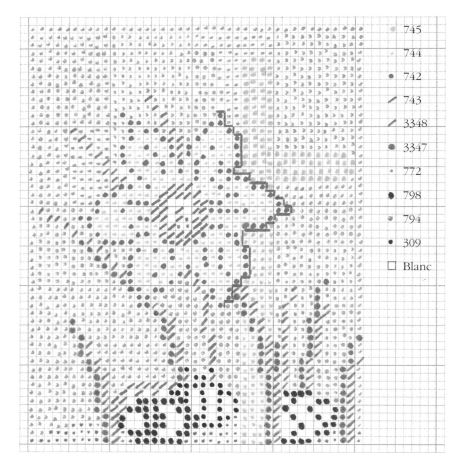

745
744
742
743
3348
3347
772
798
794
309
Blanc

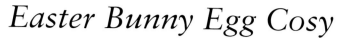

Easter Bunny Egg Cosy

Will the Easter Bunny be visiting your house this year?
Delight a child with this funny rabbit egg cosy

DESIGN SIZE 3¼ x 4in (8.3 x 10cm)
STITCH Tent stitch

□ Needle, size 22
□ Canvas 18 holes per inch (7 holes per centimetre), 6 x 6in (15 x 15cm)
□ Stranded cottons (floss) as listed on chart key. Use three strands of thread unless stated otherwise
□ Backing fabric (cotton), three pieces 6in (15cm) square

□ Two pieces of wadding (batting), ½in thick, each one 5in (12.7cm) square

DMC	COLOUR	ANCHOR
798	Blue	131
Blanc	white	01
800	Sky blue	128
3078	Lemon	292
3326	Pale pink	25
818	Very pale pink	48
317	Dark grey	400

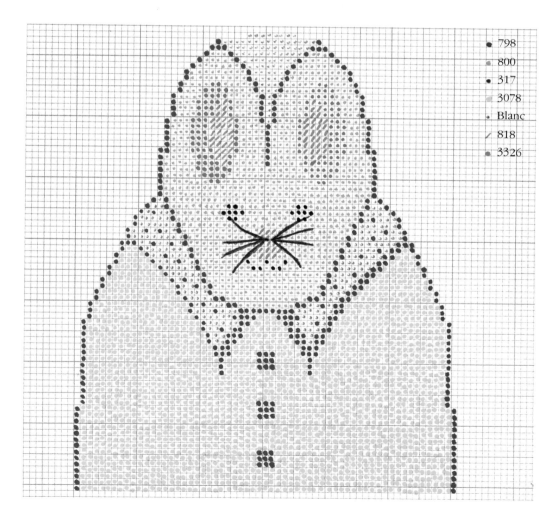

●	798
▨	800
•	317
▨	3078
·	Blanc
╱	818
●	3326

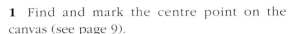

1 Find and mark the centre point on the canvas (see page 9).

2 Count from the centre point to the base of the bunny's chin and start stitching here. Work colour by colour.

3 Using one strand of dark grey, oversew the whiskers.

4 Block your needlepoint (following the instructions on page 17).

5 Place the needlepoint and one piece of the backing fabric right sides together. Using a suitably coloured cotton thread, backstitch as close to the edge of the design as possible to attach the backing fabric to the canvas. Leave the base open. Trim to ¼ in (5mm) from the edge of the stitching. Turn the right way out and press gently. Cut out two pieces of wadding (batting) to fit. Insert one between the canvas and the backing fabric. Tuck under the remaining raw edges of material and sew up neatly.

6 Using the outline of the chart as a template, and allowing for a small seam allowance, cut two rabbit shapes from the remaining pieces of cotton fabric. Sew around the edges leaving the base open. Turn inside out. Insert the second piece of wadding (batting) inside this rabbit. Sew up the base.

7 With wrong sides together, very neatly sew round the outside edge of the two rabbits, leaving the base open.

Easter card (page 28), and the Easter Bunny and Duck Egg Cosies.

Duck Egg Cosy

Smart bow tie, best bib and tucker, shiny beaked and bright eyed,
this comic duck would make a perfect partner to the
Easter Bunny egg cosy

DESIGN SIZE 3¼ x 4in (8.2 x 10 cm)
STITCH Tent stitch

□ The materials required are the same as for the Easter Bunny Egg Cosy (see page 29)

1 Find and mark the centre point on the canvas (see page 9).
2 Count from the centre point to the base of the duck's head and start stitching here. Work colour by colour.

3 Block your needlepoint (see page 17).
4 Complete the egg cosy by following steps 5 to 7 on page 30.

DMC	COLOUR	ANCHOR
744	Yellow	301
972	Dark yellow	298
700	Green	244
608	Orange	330
606	Dark orange	334
310	Black	403
Blanc	White	01

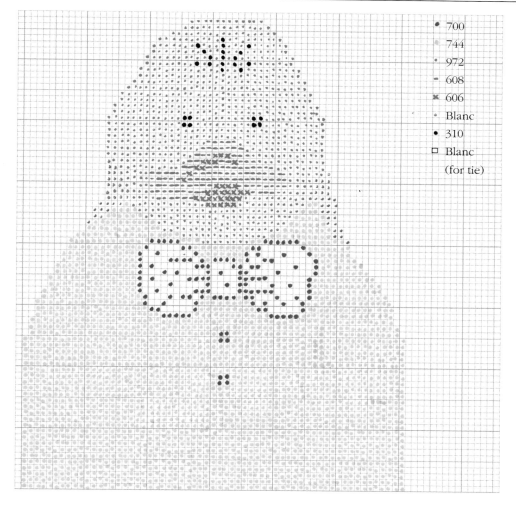

●	700
⋮	744
∴	972
−	608
✕	606
·	Blanc
●	310
□	Blanc (for tie)

Chequered Frame

Soft spring shades of blue and peach create a pair of frames suitable for mirrors or treasured photographs. Experiment with different colours to suit your own room

DESIGN SIZE 3¾ x 4¾in (9.5 x 12cm)
STITCHES Tent stitch, cushion stitch, basket-weave stitch, rhodes stitch

☐ Needle, size 22
☐ Canvas 18 holes per inch (7 holes per centimetre), 7 x 8in (17 x 20cm)
☐ Stranded cottons (floss) as listed on chart key. Use three strands of thread unless stated otherwise
☐ Cardboard frame, 3½ x 4½in (9 x 11.5cm) with an aperture 1¾ x 3in (4.4 x 7.5cm)
☐ Cardboard backing, 3½ x 4½in (9 x 11.5cm), ¼in (3mm) thick
☐ Backing fabric (calico or cotton), 7 x 8in (17 x 20cm)
☐ Mirror (if using), ¼in (3mm) thick, 1¾ x 3in (4.4 x 7.5cm)
☐ Wadding (batting), ½in (1 cm) thick, 3½ x 4½in (9 x 11.5cm)
☐ Perspex sheeting, 2½ x 3½in (6.5 x 9cm) PVA glue

1 Find and mark the centre point on the canvas (see page 9).
2 Count from the centre point to the top right-hand corner and stitch all the borders in tent stitch.
3 Work all the basketweave squares, followed by the cushion stitch squares and lastly the rhodes stitch squares.
4 Block your needlepoint (see page 17).
5 Trim the canvas to ¾in (2cm) from the edge of the stitching.
6 Glue the wadding (batting) to the front of the cardboard frame, and cut out the centre of the wadding (batting) along the inner edges of the frame.
7 Place the needlepoint reverse side down onto the wadding (batting), turn face down and glue the outer bare edges of canvas to the back

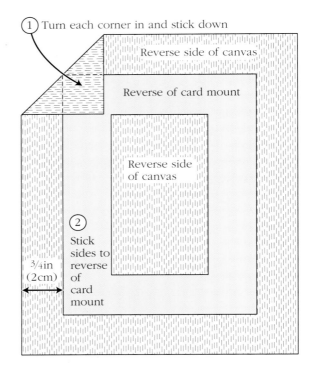

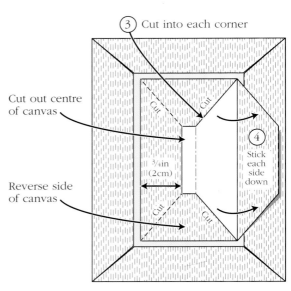

Making a frame

of the cardboard frame. See steps 1 and 2 on diagram opposite. When dry, cut out the centre piece of bare canvas, leaving a margin of ¾ in (2cm). Cut into the corners where shown and glue the inner edges of bare canvas to the back of the card. See steps 3 and 4 on diagram opposite. Take care not to leave bare canvas visible from the front.

8 Cover the backing card with the calico or cotton fabric.

9 Place your photograph or mirror centrally onto the backing board and glue down. If using a photograph, cover it with the piece of perspex to protect it from dust.

10 Place the frame right side up onto the backing board and glue the two pieces together.

11 Make a twist of threads. Choose three colours of thread and do not separate the strands. Cut each length to 150in (400cm), put them together and tie one end to a fixed point such as a hook or door handle. Twist the three threads together, keeping them taut until they begin to twist together when slightly relaxed. Then, keeping the rope taut, fold it in half, with the two loose ends together. Release the tied end and, holding both loose ends tightly, let the folded end go. The threads will wrap around one another. If there are any knots or loose sections, ease these out with your fingers and then knot the loose end of the twist.

12 Secure one end to the frame at a corner, tucking the end in between the front and back pieces. Glue the twist to the outside edge of the frame covering the bare canvas. You will need to go around twice, then secure the end by tucking it in between the front and back of the frame. Repeat this on the inside border either once or twice around, as necessary.

13 Make a small loop of twist to hang the frame and secure it at the top.

DMC	COLOUR	ANCHOR	STITCH	STRANDS
Peach Frame				
351	Dark peach	11	Cushion	4
			Tent (inner and outer borders)	4
352	Peach	9	Basketweave	3
948	Very pale peach	1011	Rhodes	3
800	Sky blue	120	Rhodes	3
Blue Frame				
792	Dark blue	941	Cushion	4
			Tent (inner and outer borders)	4
794	Blue	939	Basketweave	3
745	Cream	300	Rhodes	3
353	Pale peach	8	Rhodes	3

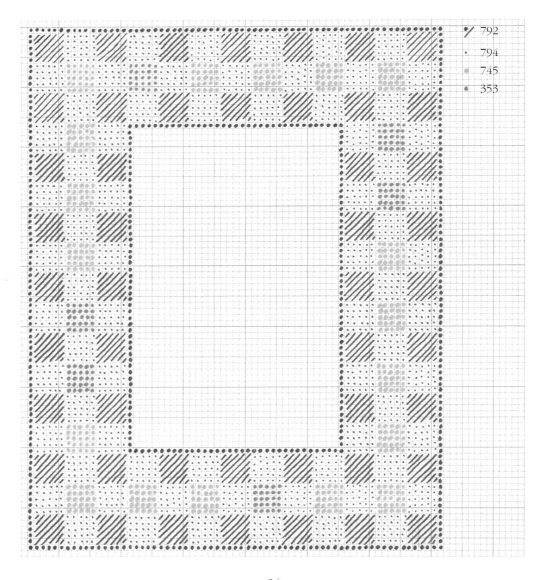

⁄	792
·	794
●	745
●	353

Balloon Sampler

A lovely idea for a child or new baby, this picture takes names up to eight letters long or initials. A good piece for practising different, uncomplicated stitches (see photograph on pages 18–19)

DESIGN SIZE 4 x 4in (10 x 10cm)
STITCHES Tent stitch, basketweave stitch, French knots, jacquard stitch, diagonal mosaic stitch, cushion stitch, cross stitch, rhodes stitch, double cross stitch, long stitch

□ Needle, size 22
□ Canvas 18 holes per inch (7 holes per centimetre), 6 x 6in (15 x 15cm)
□ Stranded cottons (floss) as listed on chart key. Use three strands of thread unless stated otherwise

1 Find and mark the centre point on the canvas (see page 9).
2 Count from the centre point to the right-hand corner of the inner border and work all the borders first.

3 Work the green and yellow hills, the trees, balloons and clouds, then fill in the sky. Using one strand of white, oversew ropes for the balloons. Using one strand of light brown, oversew the fence.
4 Work the rope border using dark green and green. Your first long stitch will use the same holes as the border tent stitch. Then work the corners in rhodes stitch using pink.
5 Using the alphabet below, and following the instructions on page 17, stitch your name or initials in the panel, working in cross stitch. Pink, green or blue would work well with the colours of the rest of the design. Fill in the background with tent stitch in white.
6 Block your needlepoint (see page 17).
7 Mount and frame as preferred. We used a ready-made shop frame.

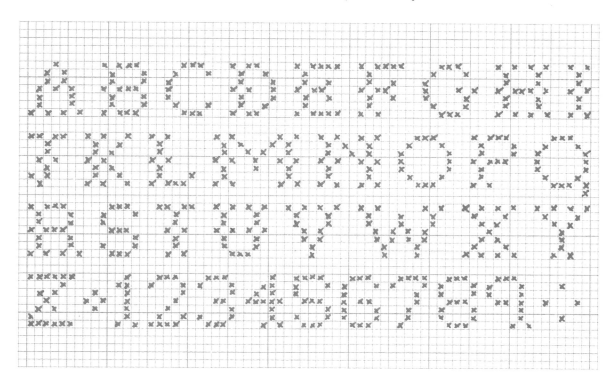

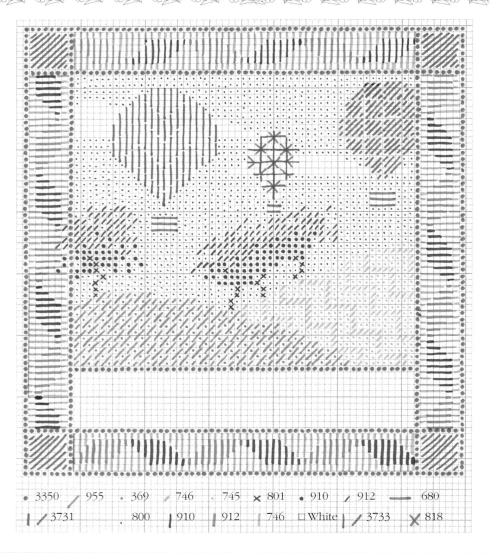

| . | 3350 | / | 955 | . | 369 | / | 746 | | 745 | × | 801 | • | 910 | / | 912 | — | 680 |
| | 3731 | | | . | 800 | | 910 | / | 912 | | 746 | □ | White | / | 3733 | × | 818 |

DMC	COLOUR	ANCHOR	STITCH	STRANDS
Blanc	White	01	Tent	3
746	Pale cream	386	Jacquard (hill)	4
			Long (outer border)	4
745	Yellow	301	Jacquard	4
955	Very light green	202	Diagonal mosaic	4
369	Pale green	1043	Diagonal mosaic	4
3350	Dark pink	78	Tent	4
3731	Mid pink	77	Cushion (right-hand balloon)	4
			Long (left-hand balloon)	4

DMC	COLOUR	ANCHOR	STITCH	STRANDS
3733	Pink	75	Cushion (right-hand balloon)	4
			Long (left-hand balloon)	4
			Double cross (middle balloon)	4
			Rhodes	4
818	Very pale pink	271	Double cross	4
910	Dark green	245	French knots (trees)	3
			(Long border)	4
912	Green	243	French knots	3
			Long (border)	4
801	Brown	359	Cross	3
800	Sky blue	120	Basketweave	3
680	Light brown	890	Long	4

Jug of Anenomes Cushion

This elegant cushion inset showing a jug of spring-flowering anenomes makes a super partner to the Crocus Bowl on page 38

DESIGN SIZE 3 x 3in (7.5 x 7.5cm)
STITCHES Tent stitch, basketweave stitch

☐ Needle, size 22
☐ Canvas 18 holes per inch (7 holes per centimetre), 6 x 6in (15 x 15cm)
☐ Stranded cottons (floss) as listed on chart key.
☐ Use three strands of thread
☐ Fabric (cotton) to make up into a cushion, 9 x 18in (23 x 46cm)
☐ Kapok
☐ White cord, ¼in x 32 in (5mm x 83 cm)
☐ Sewing Thread

DMC	COLOUR	ANCHOR
744	Yellow	301
552	Purple	99
554	Pale lilac	90
340	Mauve	108
550	Dark purple	102
211	Pale mauve	342
895	Dark green	263
471	Green	255
310	Black	403
553	Dark lilac	110
209	Lilac	97
Blanc	White	01
745	Cream	300

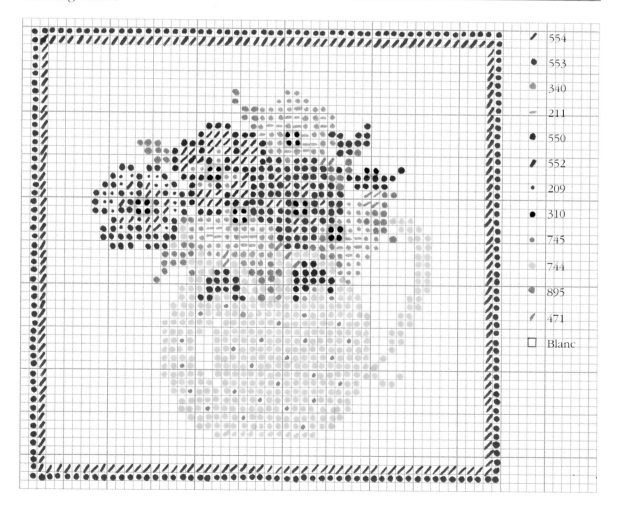

Symbol	DMC
╱	554
●	553
▪	340
╌	211
●	550
╱	552
•	209
●	310
•	745
•	744
●	895
╱	471
☐	Blanc

1 Find and mark the centre point on the canvas (see page 9).

2 Count from the centre point to the top right-hand corner of the border and start stitching here. Complete the border then work colour by colour finishing with the background in basketweave stitch. Make sure your hands are really clean before you stitch the white background!

3 Block your needlepoint (see page 17).

4 To make up into a cushion, firstly cut your fabric in half, giving two pieces 9 x 9in (25 x 25cm). Cut one piece into four equal triangles (see diagram on page 86).

5 Place one triangle right sides together with your needlepoint (see diagram on page 86). Stitch either by hand or machine along line A as close to the needlepoint stitches as possible. Repeat this for all four sides. Press the seams out gently.

6 Put right sides together and stitch from the inner corners to the outer corners of the cushion (see diagram on page 87). Press these seams out.

7 Trim the outer edge to make an 9in (25cm) square. Cut the backing fabric to the same size. Put right sides together and sew 1in (2 cm) in from the edge around the four sides of the cushion. Leave a central gap of 4in (10.2cm) on the bottom side.

8 Trim the edges to ½in (1cm) from the edge of the stitching and cut diagonally across the corners. Turn inside out and press. Fill with Kapok, pushing it well into the corners.

9 Insert one end of the cord into the opening at the centre and attach it. Sew up three-quarters of the opening, then sew the cord to the edge of the cushion. Tuck the second end of the cord into the cushion before sewing up the remaining gap.

Crocus Bowl Cushion

A springtime bowl of colourful flowering crocuses brings Clarice Cliff's classic thirties' designs to mind. Here we have used it as a delightful small cushion inset

DESIGN SIZE 3 x 3in (7.5 x 7.5cm)
STITCHES Tent stitch, basketweave stitch

☐ Needle, size 22
☐ Canvas 18 holes per inch (7 holes per centimetre), 6 x 6in (15 x 15cm)
☐ Stranded cottons (floss) as listed on chart key. Use three strands of thread
☐ Fabric (cotton) to make up into a cushion, 9 x 18in (23 x 46cm)
☐ Kapok
☐ White cord, ¼in x 32in (5mm x 83cm)
☐ Sewing thread

1 Find and mark the centre point on the canvas (see page 9).

2 Count from the centre point to the top right-hand corner of the border and start stitching here. Complete the border then work colour by colour finishing with the background in basketweave stitch. Make sure your hands are really clean before you stitch the white background!

3 Block your needlepoint (see page 17).

4 Make your finished stitching into a cushion by following steps 4 to 9 of the Jug of Anemones design above.

Opposite *The Jug of Anemones and Crocus Bowl cushions*

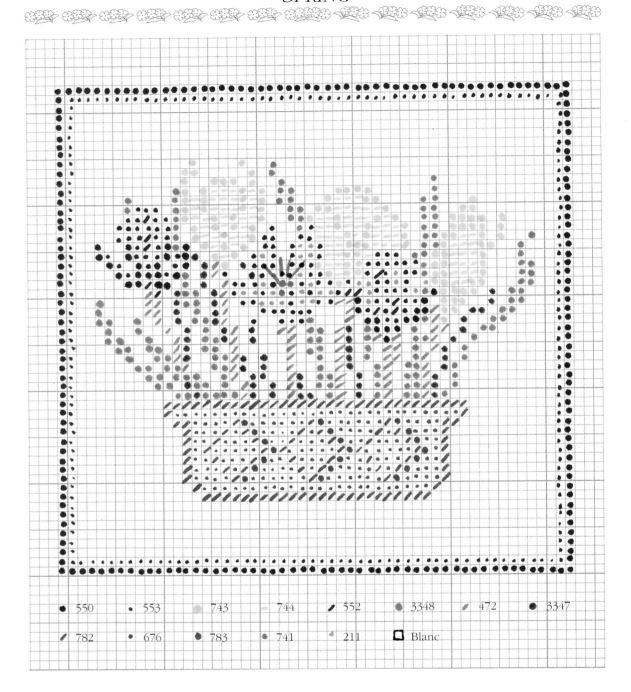

| • | 550 | • | 553 | | 743 | | 744 | / | 552 | ● | 3348 | / | 472 | ● | 3347 |

| / | 782 | • | 676 | ● | 783 | ● | 741 | ◦ | 211 | ☐ | Blanc |

DMC	COLOUR	ANCHOR
550	Dark purple	102
553	Mid purple	110
211	Pale purple	342
743	Dark yellow	303
744	Yellow	301
741	Orange	304
552	Purple	99

DMC	COLOUR	ANCHOR
472	Light green	255
3347	Green	261
3348	Mid green	262
783	Gold	1045
676	Light gold	891
782	Dark gold	1046
Blanc	White	01

Crabapple Tile

This bright design, depicting crabapple flowers, is the first of a seasonal series of 'tile' designs. Stitch them separately or work and frame them together as a single project

DESIGN SIZE 3⅝ x 3¾ (93cm x 95cm)
STITCHES Tent stitch, basketweave stitch, French knots

☐ Needle, size 22
☐ Canvas 18 holes per inch (7 holes per centimetre), 6½ x 6½ in (16 x 16cm)
☐ Stranded cottons (floss) as listed on chart key.
☐ Use three strands of thread

1 Find and mark the centre point on the canvas (see page 9).
2 Count from the centre point to the top right-hand corner of the border and start stitching here. Work the border colour by colour.

3 Work the flower details, then fill in the background in basketweave stitch.
4 Stitch the French knots on the flowers.
5 Block your needlepoint (see page 16).
6 Mount and frame as preferred. This picture was professionally mounted and framed using a lacquered wooden frame.

DMC	COLOUR	ANCHOR
471	Green	255
472	Light green	254
744	Yellow	301
309	Dark pink	39
3326	Pale pink	24
611	Brown	898
Blanc	White	01

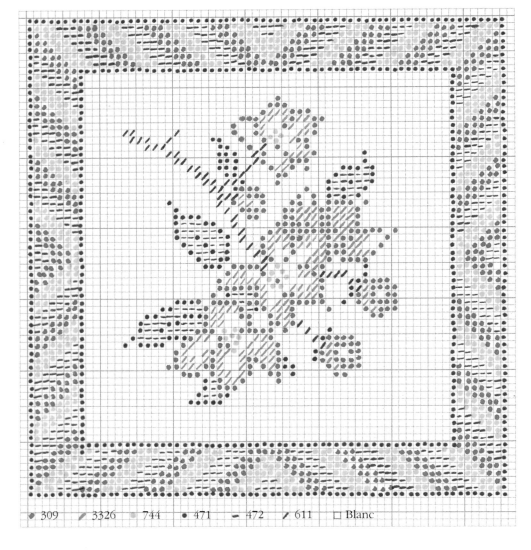

● 309 ⟋ 3326 ▌ 744 ● 471 ▬ 472 ⟋ 611 ☐ Blanc

Spring Garden Picture

Daffodils and polyanthus grow happily beneath a cherry tree in full bloom in this springtime garden. Clear blue skies and bright, fresh colours herald the coming of warmer days

DESIGN SIZE 2⅞ x 4in (7.3 x 10.3 cm)
STITCHES Tent stitch, cross stitch, French knots, long stitch, brick stitch, basketweave stitch

☐ Needle, size 22
☐ Canvas 18 holes per inch (7 holes per centimetre), 6 x 7in (15 x 17cm)
☐ Stranded cottons (floss) as listed on chart key. Use three strands of thread unless stated otherwise

1 Find and mark the centre point on the canvas (see page 9).
2 Count from the centre point to the white fence and start stitching here. Work colour by colour.
3 Using one strand of brown, oversew the distant fence. Using two strands of mid green, oversew the daffodil leaves. You may add more French knots to the cherry tree if you wish in very pale pink. Outline fence with dark green in back stitch.
4 Work the borders and the diamond outlines of the side panel in perlé. Fill in the panel following the chart in tent stitch.

5 Block your needlepoint (see page 16).
6 You can mount this picture together with the Summer, Autumn and Winter Garden scenes in one frame as shown on page 2

DMC	COLOUR	ANCHOR	STITCH
Blanc	White	01	Tent
800	Sky blue	120	Basketweave
936	Dark green	269	Tent
3346	Mid green	262	Long (daffodil leaves)
			Chain (primula leaves)
3347	Green	261	Tent
3348	Light green	264	Tent
899	Mid pink	26	French knots
818	Very pale pink	271	French knots
743	Dark yellow	302	Cross
744	Yellow	301	French knots
740	Orange	316	Tent
208	Purple	110	French knots
729	Beige	890	Brick
676	Pale beige	891	Brick
745	Cream perlé	300	Tent
801	Brown	359	Tent
772	Pale green	264	Tent
47	Burgundy	321	French knot

You may add the title 'Spring' (charted below) to the top or bottom of this design

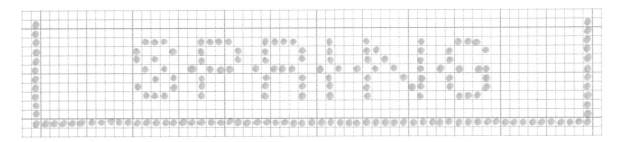

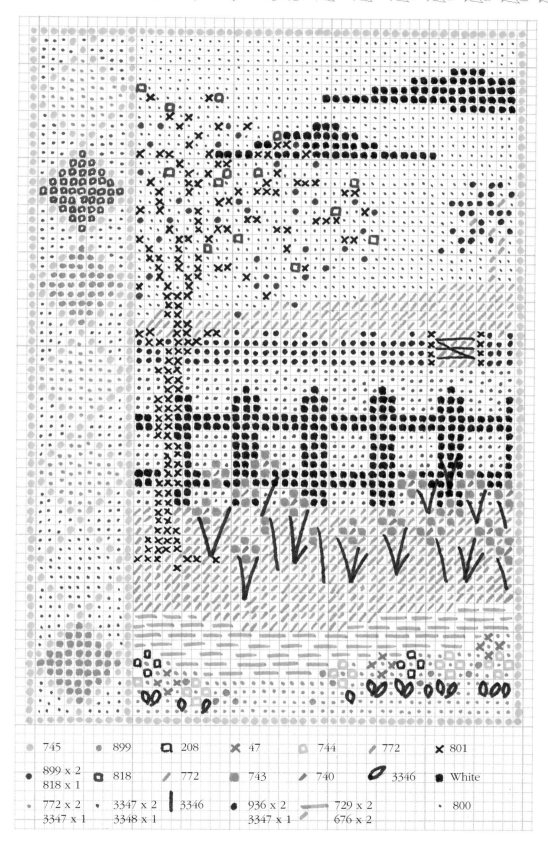

• 745	• 899	▢ 208	✕ 47	▢ 744	╱ 772	✕ 801
• 899 x 2 818 x 1	▢ 818	╱ 772	■ 743	╱ 740	⬭ 3346	⬣ White
• 772 x 2 3347 x 1	• 3347 x 2 3348 x 1	▮ 3346	• 936 x 2 3347 x 1	— 729 x 2 676 x 2		• 800

SUMMER

And I will make thee beds of roses
And a thousand fragrant posies,
A cap of flowers, and a kirtle
Embroidered all with leaves of myrtle
CHRISTOPHER MARLOWE

Summer – the season of long days in the sun, of warmth and the abundance of Nature's bounty. The projects in this chapter are full of fun, bright colours and floral abandon. The motifs conjure up the atmosphere of hot summer days in the garden, and of children playing in the fresh air. Ladybirds and beehives, butterflies, sunflowers and summer fruits decorate cards, bookmarks, picture frames and many other small projects that will give pleasure all year long. Worked in stranded cottons (floss), they are a delight to stitch, even on the warmest of days.

Sunflower Pincushion

The sunflower head makes a dramatic design that we felt was ideal for this pincushion (pictured on pages 46–47

DESIGN SIZE 3½ x 3½ in (8.9 x 8.9cm)
STITCHES Tent stitch

☐ Needle, size 22
☐ Canvas 18 holes per inch (7 holes per centimetre), 6½ x 6½ in (16 x 16cm)
☐ Stranded cottons (floss) as listed on chart key. Use three strands of thread
☐ Yellow cotton fabric to make up cushion, 6in (15cm) square
☐ Gold cord, ¼ in (3mm) thick, 18in (45cm) long
☐ Kapok

1 Find and mark the centre point on the canvas (see page 9).
2 Start stitching the middle of the flower from the centre point. Stitch the petals and leaves, colour by colour, then stitch the background.
3 Block your needlepoint (see page 17).
4 Complete your pincushion by following steps 4 to 7 of the Tartan Scissor Weight on page 106.

DMC	COLOUR	ANCHOR
743	Yellow	301
742	Gold	303
783	Ochre	308
829	Brown	906
702	Bright green	226
700	Green	244
939	Dark blue	152
995	Turquoise	410
729	Dark Gold	890

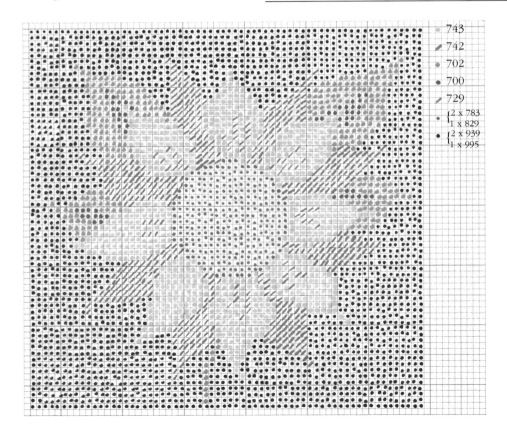

743
742
702
700
729
{2 x 783
{1 x 829
{2 x 939
{1 x 995

Beehive Picture

A little bit of nostalgia, harking back to those lazy, hazy summer days, in this warm scene of a thatched beehive in a country garden

DESIGN SIZE 3in (7.5 cm) diameter
STITCHES Tent stitch, French knots, brick stitch

□ Needle, size 22
□ Canvas 18 holes per inch (7 holes per centimetre), 6 x 6in (15 x 15cm)
□ Stranded cottons (floss) as listed on chart key. Use three strands of thread unless stated otherwise

1 Find and mark the centre point on the canvas (see page 9).
2 Count from the centre point to the top of the beehive and start stitching here. Complete the beehive, working the brick stitch of the table in brown before the background details. Using one strand of brown, outline the bottom edge of the roof in back stitch. Using two strands of orange, work the French knots.
3 Block your needlepoint (see page 17).
4 Mount and frame as preferred.

DMC	COLOUR	ANCHOR
800	Pale blue	120
792	Blue	122
772	Pale green	259
3347	Green	261
3345	Dark green	263
899	Pale pink	25
961	Pink	76
3687	Dark pink	68
869	Brown	944
782	Gold	305
743	Yellow	302
720	Orange	326
676	Pale straw	891
680	Dark straw	901
729	Straw	890
Blanc	White	01

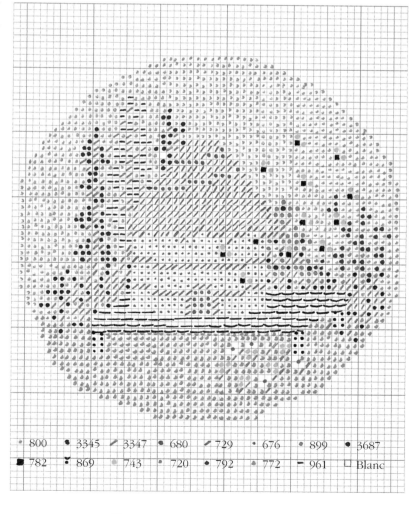

• 800	• 3345	⁄ 3347	• 680	⁄ 729	• 676	• 899	• 3687
■ 782	• 869	743	• 720	• 792	772	– 961	□ Blanc

Hollyhocks Picture

Hollyhocks are always associated with an English cottage garden in high summer, so this little picture would make ideal summer stitching

DESIGN SIZE 3¼ x 3¼ in (8.3 x 8.3cm)
STITCHES Tent stitch, basketweave stitch, cushion stitch, leaf stitch, French knots, satin stitch, cross stitch and double cross stitch.

Beehive picture (left) and hollyhocks (right)

□ Needle, size 22
□ Canvas 18 holes per inch (7 holes per centimetre), 6½ x 6½ in (16 x 16 cm)
□ Stranded cottons (floss) as listed on chart key. Use three strands of thread unless stated otherwise

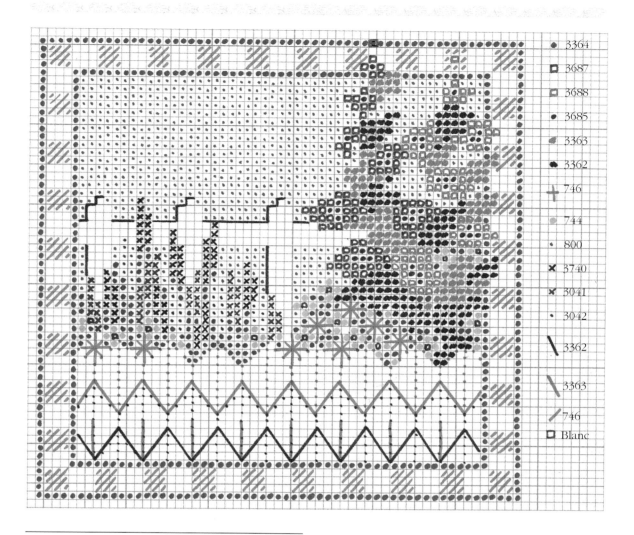

DMC	COLOUR	ANCHOR	STITCH	STRANDS
Blanc	White	01	Tent (fence)	3
			Cushion (border)	4
800	Sky blue	120	Basketweave	3
746	Pale cream	386	Cushion (border)	4
			Double cross (flowers)	3
3362	Dark green	263	Leaf (leaves)	4
			Satin (hollyhock leaves)	4
3363	Mid green	262	Leaf (leaves)	4
			Satin (hollyhock leaves)	4
3364	Light green	261	Tent	3
3687	Mid pink	75	French knots	3
3688	Pale pink	76	French knots	3
3685	Dark pink	65	Tent	3
3041	Purple	871	Cross	3
3740	Dark purple	872	Cross	3
3042	Pale purple	870	Cross	3
744	Yellow	301	Cross	4

1 Find and mark the centre point on the canvas (see page 9).

2 Count from the centre point to the white fence and start stitching here.

3 Work the details of the design, all the flower heads first, followed by the leaves, then the sky.

4 Using one strand of mid green, outline the fence in backstitch.

5 Work the border in alternate pale cream and white cushion stitches. Take care on the side borders where there is a narrow white stitch at the bottom.

6 Block your needlepoint (see page 17).

7 Mount and frame as preferred.

Cheeky Clown Bookmark

Have a jolly time stitching this Cheeky Clown bookmark (pictured on pages 46–47). It's a brilliant way to make children's reading time fun, and help them keep their place in the story

DESIGN SIZE 1⅛ x 5in (3 x 12.5 cm)
STITCHES Tent stitch

□ Needle, size 22
□ Canvas 18 holes per inch (7 holes per centimetre), 3½ x 8in (8.9 x 20cm)
□ Stranded cottons (floss) as listed on chart key. Use three strands of thread unless stated otherwise
□ Card mount, three-fold with pre-cut 1⅛ x 5in (2.8 x 12.8cm) aperture

1 Find and mark the centre point on the canvas (see page 9).
2 Count the number of stitches from the centre to the red border of the clown's tummy and start stitching here. Work colour by colour. Use a single cross stitch for the detail on the shoes and hat. Use a single French knot for the eye as shown on the chart.
3 Using one strand of red, backstitch the edge of the hat.
4 Block your needlepoint (see page 17).
5 Mount the bookmark following the instructions on page 17.

DMC	COLOUR	ANCHOR
666	Red	46
742	Gold	303
744	Yellow	301
794	Pale blue	939
820	Dark blue	134
702	Green	226
954	Light green	203
818	Pink	271
310	Black	403
Blanc	White	01

Ladybird Bookmark

Leaf stitch is used here to surround the ladybirds with rich, green foliage. This bookmark (pictured on pages 46–47) would also make a bright greetings card

DESIGN SIZE 1⅛ x 5in (3 x 12.5cm)
STITCHES Cross stitch, leaf stitch

□ Needle, size 22
□ Canvas 18 holes per inch (7 holes per centimetre), 3½ x 8in (8.9 x 20cm)
□ Stranded cottons (floss) as listed on chart key. Use three strands of thread unless stated otherwise
□ Card mount, three-fold with pre-cut 1⅛ x 5in (3 x 12.5cm) aperture

DMC	COLOUR	ANCHOR	STRANDS
666	Red	46	3
310	Black	403	3
702	Light green	242	4
701	Green	243	4
700	Dark Green	244	4

1 Find and mark the centre point on the canvas (see page 9).
2 Count from the centre point to the top right-hand corner and work the cross stitch border first in red.
3 Work the ladybirds in cross stitch.
4 Fill the background in leaf stitch, starting at

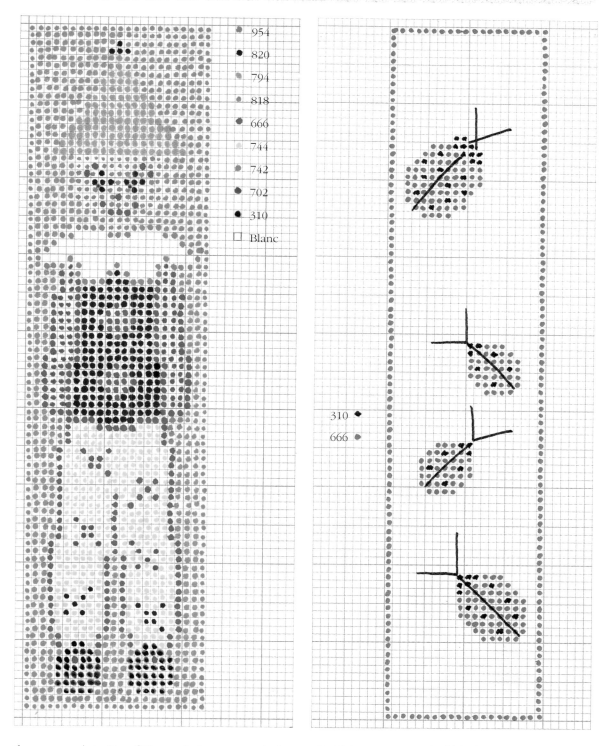

954
820
794
818
666
744
742
702
310
□ Blanc

310
666

the green dot. Use filling stitches around the ladybirds. Work approximately one third of the design in each green from dark at the bottom to light at the top, interlocking each row of leaves.

5 Using one strand of black, oversew the ladybirds' antennae, and then do the same to create the black line along their backs.

6 Make up the bookmark by following the instructions on page 17.

Strawberry Pincushion

This strawberry design was inspired by border patterns used on early nineteenth-century samplers. It is padded for use as a pincushion but can also be hung as a picture

DESIGN SIZE 4½ x 4½ in (11.5 x 11.5 cm)
STITCHES Tent stitch, cross stitch, basketweave stitch

☐ Needle, size 22
☐ Canvas 18 holes per inch (7 holes per centimetre), 7½ x 7½ in (18 x 18cm)
☐ Stranded cottons (floss) as listed on chart key. Use three strands of thread
☐ Grey board ¼ in (3mm) thick 4½ x 4½ in (11.5 x 11.5cm)

☐ Wadding (batting), ½ in (1cm) thick, 4½ x 4½ in (11.5 x 11.5cm)
☐ White card, 4½ x 4½ in (11.5 x 11.5cm)
☐ PVA glue

DMC	COLOUR	ANCHOR	STITCH
746	Pale cream (2 skeins)	386	Basketweave
936	Dark green	269	Cross
3347	Green	261	Cross
3328	Light cranberry	1024	Cross
347	Cranberry	1025	Cross
783	Beige	1045	Tent
781	Dark beige	365	Tent

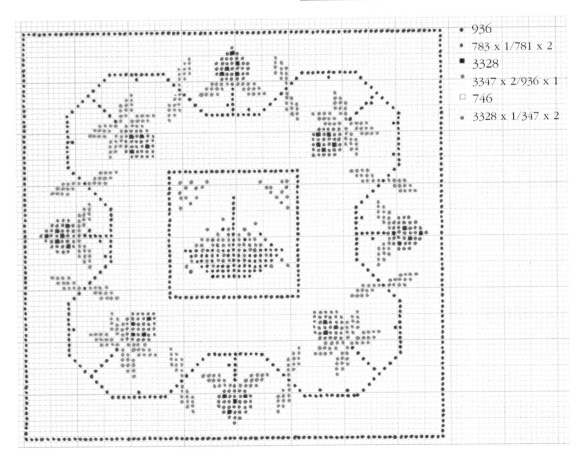

● 936
● 783 x 1/781 x 2
■ 3328
  3347 x 2/936 x 1
☐ 746
● 3328 x 1/347 x 2

1 Find and mark the centre point on the canvas (see page 9).

2 Count from the centre point to the top centre strawberry and start stitching here. Work the background last .

3 Block your needlepoint (see page 17).

4 To make into a plaque, trim the canvas to 1in (2cm) from the edge of the stitching. Stick the wadding (batting) to the board and then place the needlepoint over the wadding (batting) and turn face down. Stick the bare canvas edges to the reverse of the board, as for the Oak Leaf Door Plaque (see diagram on page 73).

5 Make a rope twist of three colours as described on page 33. Each thread should be 60in (150cm) long. Stick to the edge of the finished needlework to cover the bare edges of canvas, tucking the ends behind.

6 Cover the back of the plaque with the white card to hide the base canvas.

Strawberry Pincushion and Cherries Tile (page 56)

Cherries Tile

These rich red cherries are surely some of the loveliest of the summer fruits.

DESIGN SIZE 3⅝ x 3¾ in (9.3 x 9.5cm)
STITCHES Tent stitch, basketweave stitch

☐ Needle, size 22
☐ Canvas 18 holes per inch (7 holes per centimetre), 6½ x 6½ in (16 x 16cm)
☐ Stranded cottons (floss) as listed on chart key. Use three strands of thread

1 Find and mark the centre point on the canvas (see page 9).
2 Count from the centre point to the top right-hand corner of the border and start stitching here. Work the border colour by colour.
3 Fill in the fruit details and then the background in basketweave stitch.
4 Block your needlepoint (see page 17).
5 Mount and frame as preferred. Our picture, photographed on page 54, was professionally mounted and framed using a lacquered wooden frame.

DMC	COLOUR	ANCHOR
666	Red	46
743	Yellow	302
772	Light green	259
471	Green	255
3346	Dark green	262
3032	Brown	392
3031	Dark brown	380
816	Burgundy	20
Blanc	White	01

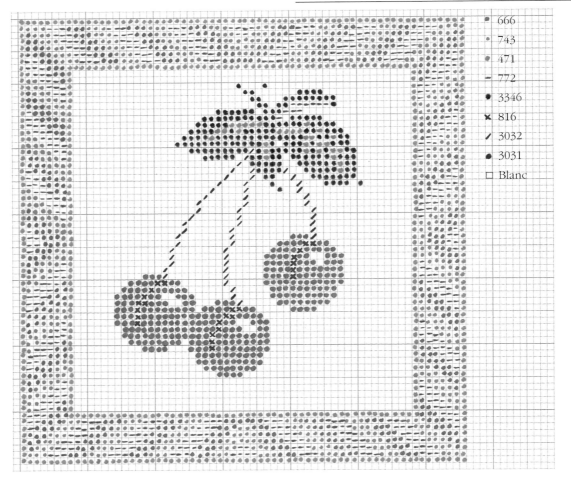

- ● 666
- • 743
- ● 471
- – 772
- ● 3346
- ✕ 816
- ／ 3032
- ● 3031
- ☐ Blanc

Gingham Hair Bow

Either of these pretty bows makes a delightful accessory to a fresh cotton summer dress. They can also be worked in any other colour to match your chosen outfit

DESIGN SIZE Each bow, 2½ x 4¾ in (6.5 x 12cm)

STITCHES Tent stitch, basketweave stitch

☐ Needle, size 22

☐ Canvas 18 holes per inch (7 holes per centimetre), for each bow 6 x 8¼ in (15 x 21cm)

☐ Barrette hair clip, 2¼ in (6cm), for each bow

☐ Stranded cottons (floss) as listed on chart key. Use three strands of thread

☐ Backing fabric (cotton or silk), pink or blue 6 x 8in (15 x 20cm)

☐ Wadding (batting) ½ in (1cm) thick, 2½ x 4¾ in (6.5 x 12cm)

1 Find and mark the centre point on the canvas (see page 9).

2 Count from the centre point to the top right-hand corner of the design and start stitching here. The white and solid blue (pink) squares are worked in basketweave stitch, and the chequered blue (pink) and white squares are worked in tent stitch.

3 Block your needlepoint (see page 16).

4 Place the needlepoint right sides together with the backing fabric. Stitch around three sides, leaving one short side open, as close to the worked needlepoint as possible using backstitch or by machine.

Gingham Hair Bow and Chequered Buttons (page 59)

5 Trim the canvas to ¼ in (5mm) from the edge of the stitching. Cut the corners diagonally and turn the right way out. Press out gently especially into the corners. Push the wadding (batting) inside and sew up the opening.

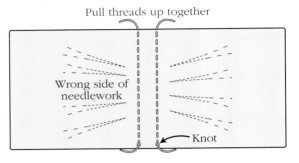

Making a bow

6 Using three strands of thread, sew a row of running stitches down the centre of the bow then, securing one end, pull the other to gather the bow evenly. Secure the second end. Make a twist of thread as described in step 11, page 33 using three threads 20in (50 cm) long and tie this around the centre of the bow. Sew the Barrette hair clip to the centre back of the bow.

DMC	COLOUR	ANCHOR
Blue (Pink) Bow		
Blanc	White	01
341 (605)	Pale blue (pale pink)	117 (55)
793 (603)	Blue (pink)	118 (57)

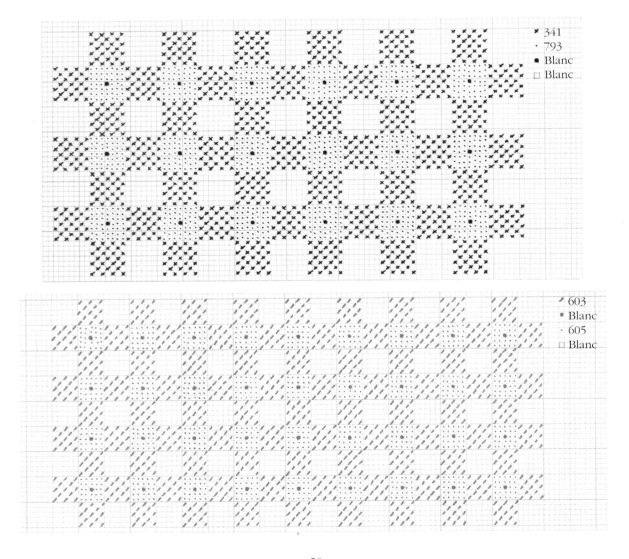

✱ 341
· 793
● Blanc
□ Blanc

✱ 603
● Blanc
· 605
□ Blanc

Chequered Buttons

These three bright and breezy buttons use the same design in different colourways making them suitable for many cardigans or jackets

DESIGN SIZE 1⅛in (2.9cm) diameter
STITCHES Tent stitch

□ Needle, size 22
□ Canvas 18 holes per inch (7 holes per centimetre), for each button 4 x 4in (10 x 10 cm)
□ Stranded cottons (floss) as listed on chart key.
□ Use three strands of thread
□ Metal buttons size 3, – 1⅛in (29mm)

1 Find and mark the centre point on the canvas (see page 9).
2 Work the centre square first and then complete the other squares. Trim the canvas to ⅛in (3mm) from the edge of the stitching.
3 Block your needlepoint (see page 17).
4 Follow metal button maker's instructions for clamping button canvas into place.

DMC	COLOUR	ANCHOR
Blue Buttons		
791	Blue	178
792	Pale blue	177
Red Buttons		
666	Red	46
321	Dark red	47
Green Buttons		
702	Green	226
701	Dark green	227
and for each button		
Blanc	White	01
744	Yellow	302

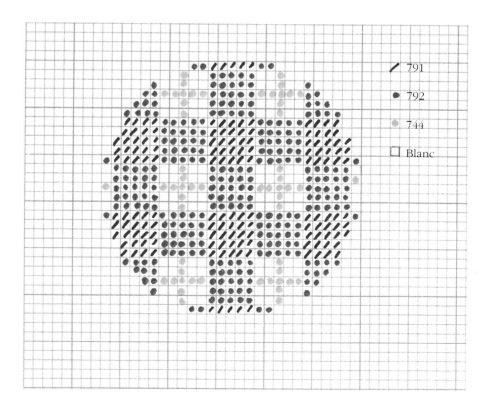

╱	791
●	792
●	744
□	Blanc

Wedding Frame

This pretty frame of summer roses lets you record the details of a special wedding. Change the colour of the initials and cord for other anniversaries

DESIGN SIZE 6¾ x 5¼ in (17 x 13.5cm)
STITCHES Tent stitch, basketweave stitch, cross stitch

☐ Needle, size 22
☐ Canvas 18 holes per inch (7 holes per centimetre), 9 x 11in (23 x 29cm)
☐ Stranded cottons (floss) and metallic thread as listed on chart key. Use three strands of thread unless stated otherwise
☐ Cardboard frame, 6½ x 5in (16.5 x 13cm) with an aperture 4⅝ x 3⅛ in (12 x 8cm)
☐ Cardboard backing, 6½ x 5in (16.5 x 13cm)

☐ Backing fabric (calico or cotton), 9 x 7in (23 x 19 cm)
☐ Wadding (batting) ½in (1cm) thick, 6½ x 5in (17 x 13cm)
☐ Silver cord, ¼ x 48in (3mm x 125cm)
☐ Perspex sheeting 5½ x 4in (15 x 10cm)
☐ PVA glue

1 Find and mark the centre point on the canvas (see page 9).
2 Count from the centre point to the inner right-hand corner and work the inner border, then the outer and the initials and details borders.

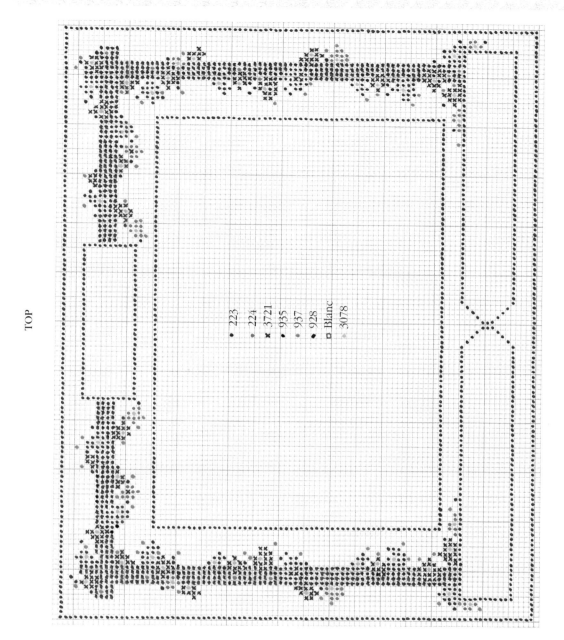

TOP

223
224
3721
935
937
928
Blanc
3078

3 Using the alphabet on page 126, and following the instructions on page 16, stitch your details into the boxes, working in tent stitch with silver metallic thread. Fill the background in tent stitch in dark rose pink.

4 Work the flowers, leaves and trellis, then fill in the white background. Using one strand of green, edge the trellis in backstitch.

5 Block your needlepoint (see page 17).

6 To make up the frame follow the instructions on page 32.

DMC	COLOUR	ANCHOR	STITCH
Blanc	White	01	Basketweave
3721	Dark rose pink	274	Cross
223	Rose pink	895	Cross
		x 2 skeins	
224	Pale rose pink	894	Cross
3078	Lemon	292	Cross
928	Grey	848	Tent
937	Green	268	Tent
935	Dark green	269	Tent
Madeira	Metallic silver		Tent

Noah's Ark Card

This cheerful greetings card (pictured on pages 46–47) uses all the bright colours of summer under a tropical sun

DESIGN SIZE 3⅛ x 3¼ in (7.9 x 8.2cm)
STITCHES Tent stitch, cross stitch, basketweave stitch, chain stitch, large cross stitch

☐ Needle, size 22
☐ Canvas 18 holes per inch (7 holes per centimetre), 6 x 6in (15 x 15cm)
☐ Stranded cottons (floss) as listed on chart key. Use three strands of thread unless stated otherwise
☐ Card mount, three-fold with pre-cut 3⅛ x 3¼in (7.9 x 8.2cm) aperture

DMC	COLOUR	ANCHOR	STITCH	STRANDS
995	Dark turquoise	410	Basketweave	3
996	Turquoise	433	Basketweave	3
954	Light green	203	Tent (ark)	3
			Chain (palm trees)	3
208	Purple	110	Large cross and tent	4
742	Gold	303	Tent and cross	3
801	Brown	359	Tent	3
970	Orange	329	Tent	3
351	Peach	10	Tent	3
349	Dark peach	13	Tent	3
823	Dark blue	148	Tent	3
Blanc	White	01	Long	1

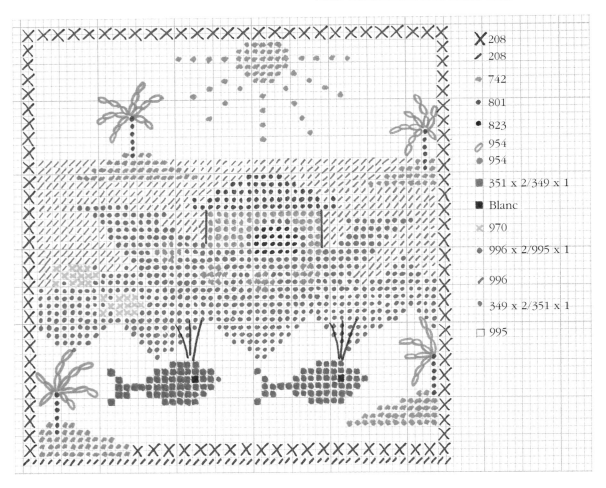

✗	208
╱	208
•	742
•	801
■	823
•	954
●	954
■	351 x 2/349 x 1
■	Blanc
✕	970
●	996 x 2/995 x 1
╱	996
•	349 x 2/351 x 1
☐	995

1 Find and mark the centre point on the canvas (see page 9).

2 Count from the centre point to the roof of the ark and start stitching here.

3 Work the details first, then fill in the sky and sea. Using one strand of white, oversew the whales' spouts. Work the leaves of the palm trees in green chain stitch. Work the outside border.

4 Block your needlepoint (see page 17).

5 Make up the card by following the instructions on page 17.

Oriental Butterfly Card

A delicate butterfly card design adapted from a piece of antique Chinese silk, our oriental butterfly is worked in a range of soft, gentle hues

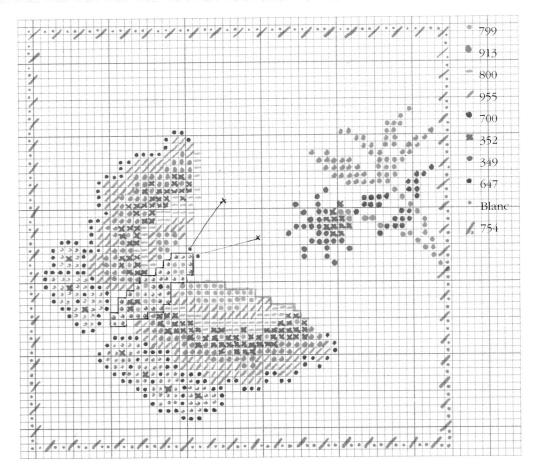

	799
	913
	800
	955
	700
	352
	349
	647
	Blanc
	754

DESIGN SIZE 3⅛ x 3¼ in (7.9 x 8.2 cm)
STITCHES Tent stitch, diagonal mosaic stitch

☐ Needle, size 22
☐ Beading needle
☐ Canvas 18 holes per inch (7 holes per centimetre), 6 x 6 in (15 x 15cm)
☐ Stranded cottons (floss) as listed on chart key. Use three strands of thread unless stated otherwise
☐ Two tiny glass seed beads in blue
☐ Card mount, three-fold with pre-cut 3⅛ x 3¼ in (7.9 x 8.2 cm) aperture

1 Find and mark the centre point on the canvas (see page 9).
2 Count from the centre point to the top of the grey outside edge of the butterfly and start stitching here. Work colour by colour.
3 Work the background in diagonal mosaic stitch.

4 Using one strand of dark blue, outline the body of the butterfly in backstitch. Using one strand of blue, oversew the antennae.
5 Block your needlepoint (see page 17).
6 Using one strand of blue, attach the glass beads where indicated on the chart.
7 Make up the card by following the instructions on page 17.

DMC	COLOUR	ANCHOR
955	Pale green	240
913	Green	242
700	Bright green	228
800	Pale blue	120
799	Blue	145
797	Dark blue	131
352	Peach	9
349	Dark peach	13
647	Grey	8581
754	Pale peach	6
Blanc	White	01

Summer Garden Picture

*Herbaceous borders, full of traditional cottage garden flowers, frame a
white wicket gate in this corner of the summer garden, giving a view
to hills beyond*

	745		772	✖	792	✖	793		3347	✖	208		743
✖	744		335	✖	47	—	209		899	✖	Blanc	•	3347 x 1 3346 x 2
•	772 x 2 3347 x 1	•	936 x 2 3346 x 1	✖	772 x 2 3347 x 1		745		729	╱	3347 x 2 772 x 1
							800	—	729 x 2 676 x 2

DESIGN SIZE 2 ⅞ x 4in (7.3 x 10cm)

STITCHES Tent stitch, cross stitch, French knots, brick stitch, basketweave stitch, flower stitch

☐ Needle, size 22

☐ Canvas 18 holes per inch (7 holes per centimetre), 6 x 7in (15 x 17cm)

☐ Stranded cottons (floss) as listed on chart key. Use three strands of thread unless stated otherwise in the instructions

1 Find and mark the centre point on the canvas (see page 9).

2 Count from the centre point to the white gate and start stitching here. Work colour by colour.

3 Using one strand of beige, oversew the distant fence.

4 Work the borders and the diamond outlines of the side panel in perlé. Fill in the panel in tent stitch following the chart.

5 Block your needlepoint (see page 16).

6 You can mount this picture together with the Spring, Autumn and Winter Garden scenes in one frame as shown on page 2.

DMC	COLOUR	ANCHOR	STITCH
Blanc	White	01	Tent
800	Sky blue	120	Basketweave
936	Dark green	269	Tent
3346	Mid green	262	Tent
3347	Green	261	Tent (grass)
			French knots (lupin leaves)
772	Light green	264	Tent
335	Pink	38	French knots
899	Mid pink	25	French knots
793	Pale blue	121	Cross
792	Dark blue	122	Cross
743	Dark yellow	302	Tent
744	Yellow	301	Cross/French knots
729	Beige	890	Brick
676	Pale beige	891	Brick
745	Cream perlé	300	Tent
208	Dark purple	110	Tent
209	Purple	109	Tent
47	Burgundy	321	Tent
745	Cream	300	Tent

You may add the title 'Summer' (charted below) to the top or bottom of this design

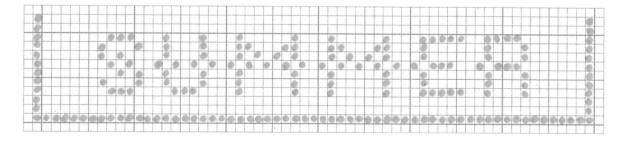

AUTUMN

Fall, leaves, fall; die, flowers, away;
Lengthen night and shorten day;
Every leaf speaks bliss to me
Fluttering from the autumn tree

EMILY BRONTË

Autumn – the season of golden colours, trees laden with berries, ripening fruit in the orchards, harvest festivals and flowers and herbs drying for winter decorations. The changing colours of autumn are all reflected in the projects for this chapter. A "marmalade" cat sits on a plush velvet cushion, and the patchwork cushion is worked in numerous autumnal hues. The little pig in her green dress and garland of russet apples makes a fun birthday card. Looking forward to Christmas, stitch the crinolined lady spectacle case and matching box lid for a really special gift.

Marmalade Cat Picture

*Warm and secure, a ginger Tom sits peacefully on the window seat
looking out over the blustery autumn garden. Deep reds and greens suggest
the coming apple harvest (pictured on pages 68–69)*

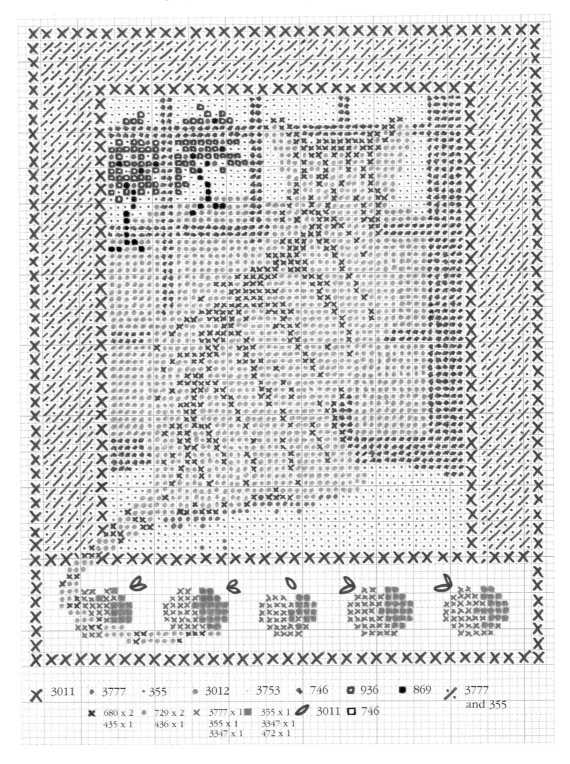

✗ 3011	• 3777	• 355	• 3012	· 3753	◆ 746	◘ 936	■ 869	✗ 3777 and 355

✗ 680 x 2	● 729 x 2	✗ 3777 x 1	■ 355 x 1	⬋ 3011	◻ 746
435 x 1	436 x 1	355 x 1	3347 x 1		
		3347 x 1	472 x 1		

DMC	COLOUR	ANCHOR	STITCH	STRANDS
936	Dark green	269	Tent	3
3011	Green	845	Large cross	4
3012	Olive green	855	Tent	3
3347	Light green	267	Tent	3
472	Lime green	254	Tent	3
3753	Pale blue	1032	Tent	3
3777	Dark wine red	1014	Diagonal mosaic (border) Tent (cushion)	4

DMC	COLOUR	ANCHOR	STITCH	STRANDS
355	Wine red	5975	Diagonal mosaic (border) Tent (cushion)	4
680	Tan	365	Tent	3
729	Light tan	363	Tent	3
436	Light camel	1045	Tent	3
435	Camel	1046	Tent	3
869	Brown	889	Tent	3
746	Cream	386	Tent	3

DESIGN SIZE 3⅞ x 5⅛ in (9.7 x 13.3cm)
STITCHES Tent stitch, large cross stitch, diagonal mosaic stitch, French knots

☐ Needle, size 22
☐ Canvas 18 holes per inch (7 holes per centimetre), 6 x 8in (15 x 20cm)
☐ Stranded cottons (floss) as listed on chart key. Use three strands unless stated otherwise

1 Find and mark the centre point on the canvas (see page 9).

2 Count from the centre point to the top of the cat's head and start stitching here.

3 Outline the left side of the cat in back stitch and oversew whiskers using one strand of brown.

4 Using three strands of wine red, work French knots for the apples. Outline windows with one strand of green. Work chain stitches in green for leaves.

5 Block your needlepoint (see the instructions given on page 17).

6 Mount and frame as preferred.

Golden Trellis Frame

English Flower Threads are a delight to work with. They are used to make a little frame in three shades of old gold (pictured on pages 68–69).

DESIGN SIZE 4¼ x 3¼ in (11 x 8.3cm)
STITCHES Rice stitch, sloping gobelin stitch, cushion stitch

☐ Needle, size 22
☐ Canvas 18 holes per inch (7 holes per centimetre), 8 x 7in (20 x 18cm)
☐ English Flower Threads and metallic threads as listed on key. Use two strands of thread
☐ Cardboard frame, 4 x 3⅛ in (10.2 x 8cm) with an aperture 2¼ x 1¼ in (5.8 x 3.3cm)
☐ Cardboard backing, 4 x 3⅛ in (10.2 x 8cm)
☐ Backing fabric (calico or cotton), 8 x 7in (20 x 18cm)
☐ Wadding (batting), 4 x 3⅛ in (10.2 x 8cm)
☐ Gold cord, ⅛ x 48in (3mm x 120cm) long
☐ PVA glue

1 Mark the centre of the canvas (see page 9).
2 Count from the centre point to the top right-hand corner and work the rice stitches across to the left. Work the large crosses first in one colour and then go back over them in the second. Make sure you leave the spaces for the metallic cushion stitches as shown on the chart.
3 Work the inner and outer borders in sloping gobelin stitch.
4 Block your needlepoint (see page 17).
5 Make up the frame (see page 32).

ENGLISH FLOWER THREADS
Dark gold
Mid gold
Light gold
Madeira Metallic Thread

ENGLISH FLOWER THREADS

Dark gold under mid gold

Mid gold under light gold

Madeira metallic gold

Dark gold

Oak Leaf Door Plaque

This autumnal door plaque will take any name up to eleven letters and is very easy to assemble. It makes a lovely gift for a child

DESIGN SIZE 6½ x 2⅜ in (16.5 x 5.5cm)
STITCHES Tent stitch, basketweave stitch, cross stitch

☐ Needle, size 22
☐ Canvas 18 holes per inch (7 holes per centimetre), 10 x 6in (25 x 15cm)
☐ Stranded cottons (floss) as listed on chart key. Use three strands of thread unless stated otherwise
☐ Cardboard backing, ¼in (3mm) thick, 6½ x 2 ⅜ in (16.5 x 5.5cm)
☐ Wadding (batting), ½in (5mm) thick, 6½ x 2 ⅜ in (16.5 x 5.5cm)
☐ Backing fabric (calico), 8½ x 4in (20.5 x 10cm)
☐ PVA glue

DMC	COLOUR	ANCHOR	STRANDS
434	Brown	370	4
435	Pale brown	369	3
780	Gold	309	3
921	Rust	339	3
937	Green	268	4
746	Pale cream	386	3

1 Find and mark the centre point on the canvas (see page 9).
2 Count from the centre point to the top right-hand corner and work the borders in tent stitch.
3 Work the oak leaves in tent stitch.
4 Using the alphabet on page 95, and following the instructions on page 17, stitch the name in cross stitch.
5 Work the background in basketweave stitch.
6 Block your needlepoint (see page 17).
7 Glue the wadding (batting) to the front of the card. Stretch the blocked needlepoint over the wadding (batting) and turn face down. Glue the bare canvas edges to the back of the board (see below).
8 Tuck the edges of the backing fabric under to give a piece the same size as the boarded needlepoint. Glue to the back of the board covering the bare canvas edges.
9 Make a rope twist of gold, green and rust as described on page 33. Each thread should be 60in (150cm) long. Glue to edge of plaque, tucking in the ends.

DOOR PLAQUE

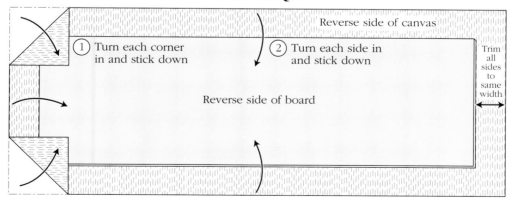

Making up the door plaque

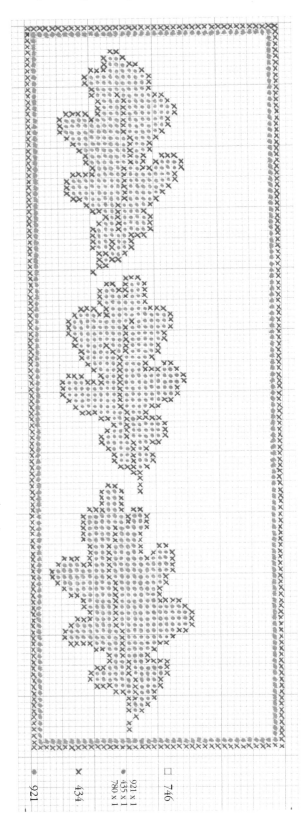

921

× 434

□ 746

921 x 1
435 x 1
780 x 1

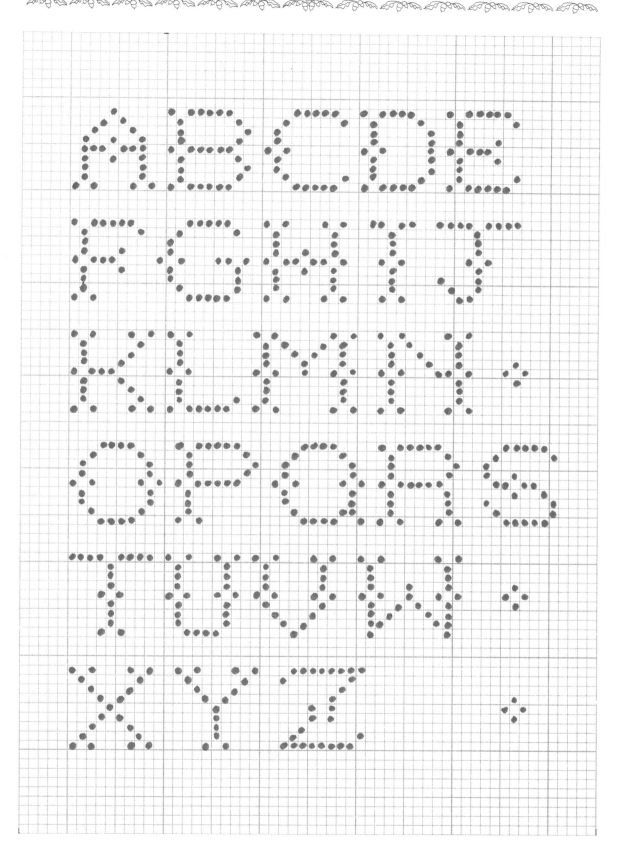

Autumn Scene Picture

This autumnal country scene makes use of a selection of different stitches to create a variety of textures

DESIGN SIZE 3⅛ x 3⅛in (7.8 x 7.8cm)
STITCHES Tent stitch, cross stitch, jacquard stitch, diagonal mosaic stitch, French knots, chain stitch, diagonal stitch

☐ Needle, size 22
☐ Canvas 18 holes per inch (7 holes per centimetre), 6 x 6in (15 x 15cm)
☐ Stranded cottons (floss) as listed on chart key. Use three strands unless stated otherwise

1 Find and mark the centre point on the canvas (see page 9).
2 Count from the centre point to the right-hand corner of the inside border and start stitching here. Work the border in tent stitch.
3 Work the details of the scene colour by colour. Using one strand of brown, oversew the distant fence.
4 Using four strands, work the outside border in diagonal stitch.

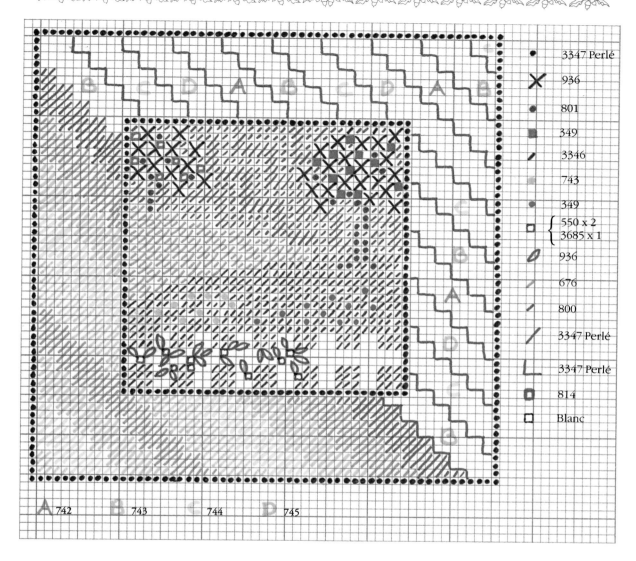

•	3347 Perlé
✕	936
•	801
■	349
/	3346
•	743
•	349
□	{550 x 2 / 3685 x 1}
⬭	936
	676
/	800
/	3347 Perlé
⌐	3347 Perlé
▢	814
▢	Blanc

A 742   B 743   C 744   D 745

5 Using one strand of mid green, outline the diagonal stitches in the top right half of the border in backstitch.

6 Block your needlepoint (see the instructions given on page 17).

7 Mount and frame as preferred.

DMC	COLOUR	ANCHOR	STITCH
3346	Mid green	262	Tent
3347	Mid green	261	Tent
Perle 5			Diagonal (inside border)
814	Red	22	French knots (tree) / Cross (flowers)
349	Dark peach	13	French knots
800	Sky blue	120	Jacquard
676	Beige	891	Diagonal mosaic
Blanc	White	01	Tent

DMC	COLOUR	ANCHOR	STITCH
742	Gold	303	Diagonal
743	Dark yellow	302	Diagonal
744	Yellow	301	Diagonal
745	Cream	300	Diagonal
801	Brown	351	Cross
936	Dark green	269	Large cross (trees) / Chain (leaves)
550	Purple	102	French knots
3685	Burgundy	70	French knots

A Bunch of Herbs Cushion

This bunch of herbs was picked from the garden and would transform an existing cushion cover if stitched on to the front and decorated with a piece of braid

DESIGN SIZE 5½ x 3⅓ in (14 x 8.5cm)
STITCHES Tent stitch, basketweave

☐ Needle, size 22
☐ Canvas 18 holes per inch (7 holes per centimetre), 8½ x 6½ in (21.5 x 16cm)
☐ Stranded cottons (floss) as listed on chart key. Use three strands of thread

1 Find and mark the centre point on the canvas (see page 9).
2 Count from the centre point to the middle of the bow and start stitching here. Work the design colour by colour. Work the background in basketweave.
3 Block your needlepoint (see page 17).
4 The herb panel shown was stitched on to an existing cushion cover with a piece of braid stitched round the edge to cover the join.

DMC	COLOUR	ANCHOR
552	Dark purple	94
554	Pale purple	92
210	Lilac	109
3345	Dark green	263
905	Bright green	257
936	Very dark green	269
772	Very pale green	259
3348	Pale green	264
610	Brown	889
352	Peach	9
351	Dark peach	10
742	Gold	303
744	Yellow	301
Blanc	White	01

Blanc

352

351

610

742

744

905

3345

3348

772

936

210

554

552

Piglet with Apples Card

We're sure this little piggy, tricked out in all her finery, stayed at home.
A card or little picture for the young at heart (pictured on pages 68–69)

DESIGN SIZE 3¼ in (8.2 cm) diameter
STITCHES Tent stitch

☐ Needle, size 22
☐ Canvas 18 holes per inch (7 holes per centimetre), 6 x 6in (15 x 15cm)
☐ Stranded cottons (floss) as listed on chart key. Use three strands of thread unless stated otherwise
☐ Card mount, three-fold with pre cut 3¼ (8.3 cm) circular aperture

1 Mark the centre of the canvas (see page 9).
2 Count from the centre point to the base of the piglet's chin and start stitching here. Work colour by colour.

3 Using one strand of brown, outline the head and snout in backstitch.
4 Block your needlepoint (see page 17).
5 Make up the card (see page 17).

DMC	COLOUR	ANCHOR
666	Red	46
741	Gold	298
702	Green	226
745	Cream	300
414	Grey	398
3774	Beige	880
3779	Dark beige	882
975	Brown	349
Blanc	White	01
700	Dark green	228

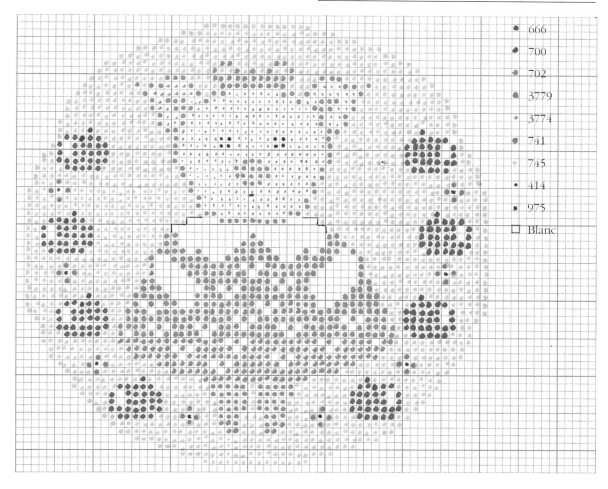

●	666
●	700
●	702
●	3779
●	3774
●	741
●	745
●	414
●	975
☐	Blanc

Crinolined Lady Trinket Box Lid

The crinolined lady, the epitome of Victorian grace and gentility, is worked on a trinket box lid to bring her charm to any dressing table

DESIGN SIZE 3½ in (8.9cm) diameter
STITCHES Tent stitch, basketweave stitch, French knots

□ Needle, size 22
□ Canvas 18 holes per inch (7 holes per centimetre), 6½ in (16cm)
□ Stranded cottons (floss) as listed on chart key. Use three strands of thread unless stated otherwise in the instructions
□ Gilt trinket box, 4in (10.2cm) diameter

DMC	COLOUR	ANCHOR
564	Pale green	206
470	Green	266
3362	Dark green	861
744	Yellow	301
722	Pale orange	323
3770	Pale peach	1011
333	Violet	119
946	Orange	332
300	Brown	371
301	Rust	349
Blanc	White	01

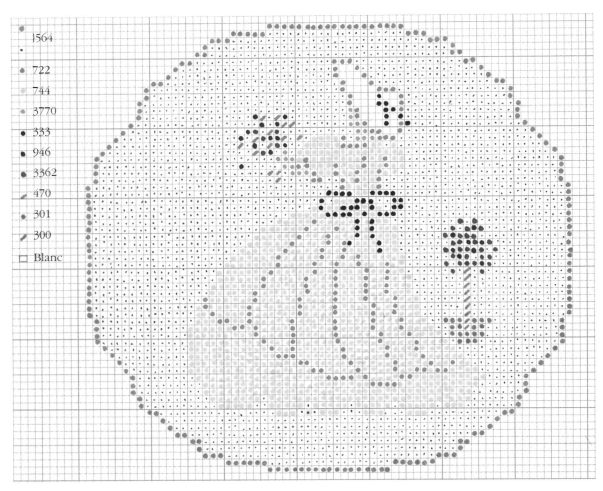

564	
722	
744	
3770	
333	
946	
3362	
470	
301	
300	
□ Blanc	

Opposite Crinolined Lady, Trinket Box Lid and Glasses Case (page 84)

1 Find and mark the centre point on the canvas (see page 9).

2 Count from the centre point to the left-hand edge of the lady's skirt and start stitching here. Work colour by colour. Fill in the background with basketweave.

3 Using two strands of violet, stitch the French knots on the lady's skirt

4 Block your needlepoint (see page 17).

5 To mount the box lid, follow the maker's instructions, trimming the canvas close to the stitching.

Crinolined Lady Glasses Case

This matching spectacles case makes the perfect complementary gift to the trinket box lid

DESIGN SIZE 3⅛ x 6¼ in (8.2 x 15.7cm)
STITCHES Tent stitch, basketweave stitch, French knots

☐ Needle, size 22
☐ Canvas 18 holes per inch (7 holes per centimetre), 6 x 9in (15 x 23cm)
☐ Stranded cottons (floss) as listed on chart key. Use three strands of thread unless stated otherwise in the instructions
☐ Backing fabric (silk or cotton), 15 x 9in (35 x 23cm) cut into three equal pieces 5 x 9in (12.5 x 23cm)
☐ Coloured cord, 12in long, ¼in (3mm) thick
☐ Wadding (batting), ½in (12cm) thick, 6½in (15.5cm) square and cut in half

1 Find and mark the centre point on the canvas (see page 9).

2 Count from the centre point to the left-hand edge of the lady's skirt and start stitching here. Work colour by colour. Fill in the background with basketweave.

3 Using two strands of violet, stitch the French knots on the lady's skirt. Using two strands of

yellow, stitch the French knots in the centre of the flowers.

4 Block your needlepoint (see page 17).

5 To make into a glasses case follow step 5 of the Easter Bunny Egg Cosy project (page 30).

6 Repeat step 5 using the two remaining pieces of backing fabric and wadding.

7 Attach cord to the inside of the bottom right-hand edge with a few stitches. With the wrong sides together, and ignoring the cord, very neatly stitch up three sides leaving the top open. Stitch the cord round the bottom and left-hand side, tucking the end into the top and anchoring with a few stitches on the inside.

DMC	COLOUR	ANCHOR
564	Pale green (2 skeins)	206
470	Green	266
3362	Dark green	861
744	Yellow	301
722	Pale orange	323
3770	Pale peach	1011
333	Violet	119
3746	Pale violet	118
946	Orange	332
Blanc	White	01

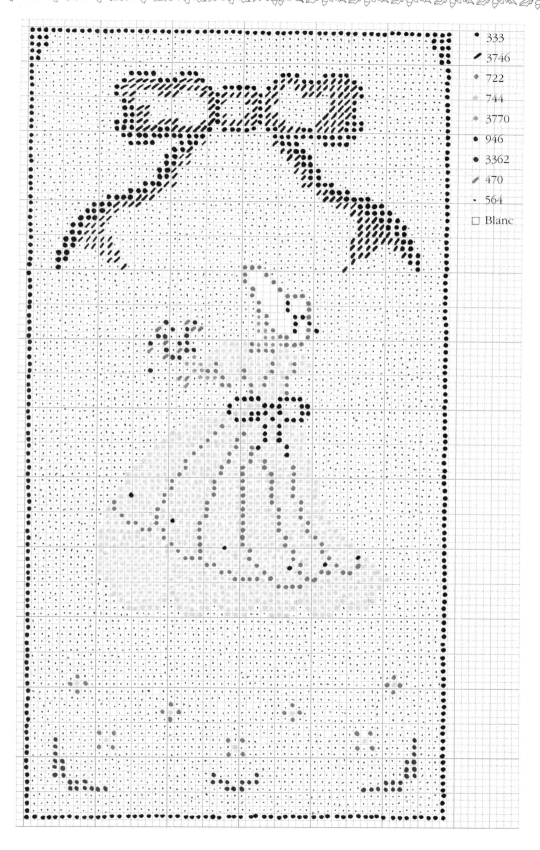

●	333
╱	3746
●	722
●	744
●	3770
●	946
●	3362
╱	470
·	564
□	Blanc

Autumn Patchwork Cushion

This cushion can be referred to time and time again as a sampler of most of the stitches in this book. Work it in different colourways to match specific decorations

DESIGN SIZE 5½ x 5½in (14 x 14cm)

STITCHES Tent stitch, cross stitch, basketweave stitch, long stitch, rhodes stitch, cushion stitch, diagonal mosaic stitch, leaf stitch, double cross stitch, byzantine stitch, eyelet stitch, broad cross stitch, large cross stitch, milanese stitch, moorish stitch, rice stitch.

☐ Needle, size 22
☐ Canvas 18 holes per inch (7 holes per centimetre), 10 x 10in (25 x 25cm)
☐ Stranded cottons (floss) as listed on chart key. Use three strands of thread unless stated otherwise
☐ Fabric (cotton or calico) to make up into a cushion, 18 x 36in (50 x 100cm)
☐ Cushion pad, 13in (32cm) square
☐ Rope cord, ¼ x 54in (½cm x 140cm)
☐ Sewing thread

1 Find and mark the centre point on the canvas (see page 9).

2 Count from the centre point to the inner cross stitch border and start stitching here. Work the cross stitch borders of the central patterned square first and then fill in the squares with the different stitch patterns as shown on the chart and the detailed photograph on page 10. Some patterns require a tent stitch border around the edge of the square and this is shown on the chart by a diagonal symbol. If you find any stitch too difficult you could replace it with another. Using the alphabet work your initials in the centre panel in cross stitch (see page 17).

3 Work the outer borders in cross stitch and then the alphabet. Using the chart on page 125 you may insert the current year after the Z. Follow the chart carefully when stitching the alphabet as, to make it fit symmetrically, there is not always the same gap between letters.

4 Work the triangle pattern border and rhodes stitch corners.

5 Block your needlepoint (see page 17).

6 To make up into a cushion, firstly cut your fabric in half, giving two pieces 18 x 18in (50 x 50cm). Cut one piece into four equal triangles.

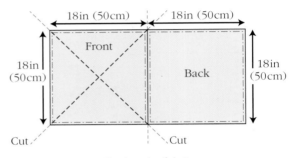

Cutting the fabric

7 Place one triangle right sides together with your needlepoint making sure that the bottom edge of the fabric, B, is parallel to the edge of the needlepoint, C, and pin. Stitch, either by hand or machine, along line A as close to the needlepoint stitches as possible. Stitch accurately to the corners of the needlepoint. Repeat this for all four sides. Press the seams out gently.

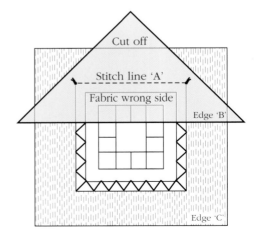

Attaching a triangle of fabric to your needlepoint

8 Place face down and, putting right sides together, stitch from each inner corner to each outer corner of the cushion, D to E (see diagram on page 88). Press these seams out.

9 Trim the outer edge of the canvas to make a 14in (35cm) square. Cut the backing fabric to the same size. Put right sides together and sew 1in (2cm) from the edge, around the four sides

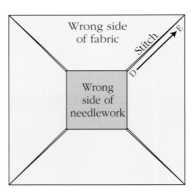

Stitching the corners

of the cushion, leaving a central gap of 6in (15cm) on the bottom side.

10 Trim the fabric to ½ in (1cm) from the edge of the stitching and cut diagonally across the corners. Turn inside out and press. Insert the cushion pad, pushing well into the corners.

11 Insert one end of cord into the opening at the centre and attach it. Sew up half the opening, then sew the cord to the edge of the cushion. Tuck the second end of cord inside the cushion before sewing up the remaining gap.

DMC	COLOUR	ANCHOR	STITCH	STRANDS
3777	Dark burgundy	1014	Cross	3
948	Pale fawn	1010	Basketweave	3
434	Brown	370	Byzantine	4
433	Mid brown	371	Moorish	4
435	Pale brown	369	Rhodes	3
977	Pale tan	363	Cushion	4
758	Rose pink	894	Double cross	4
976	Tan	1001	Tent and cushion (inner border)	4
			Long (outer border)	4
721	Pale orange	1003	Eyelet	3
920	Rust	1004	Diagonal mosaic	4
402	Camel	1047	Leaf	4
3722	Dark plum	1027	Broad cross	4
356	Mid dusky pink	339	Rice	4
			Rhodes (corners)	3
676	Pale beige	311	Milanese	4
			Long (outer border)	4
3778	Dusky pink	1013	Large cross	4
			Rhodes	3

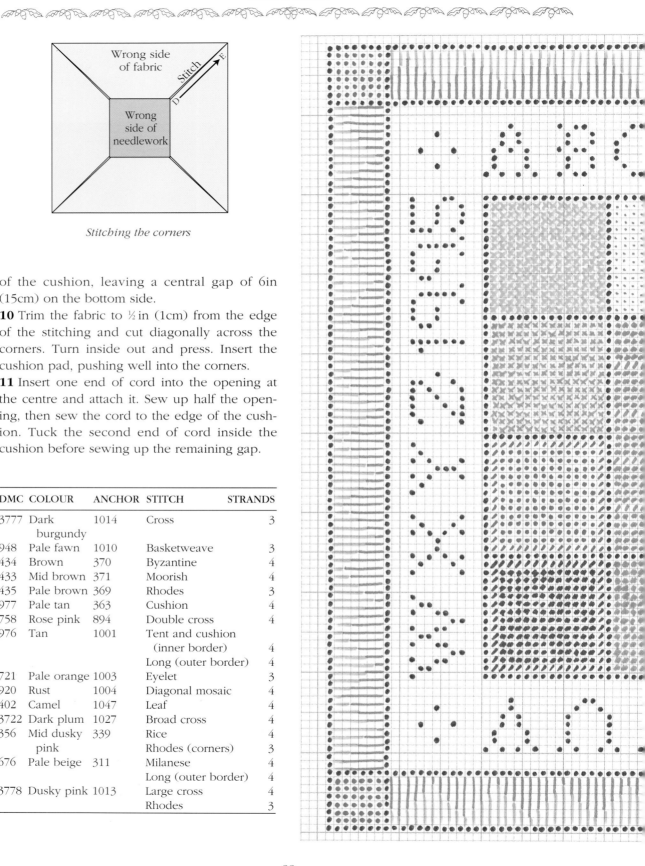

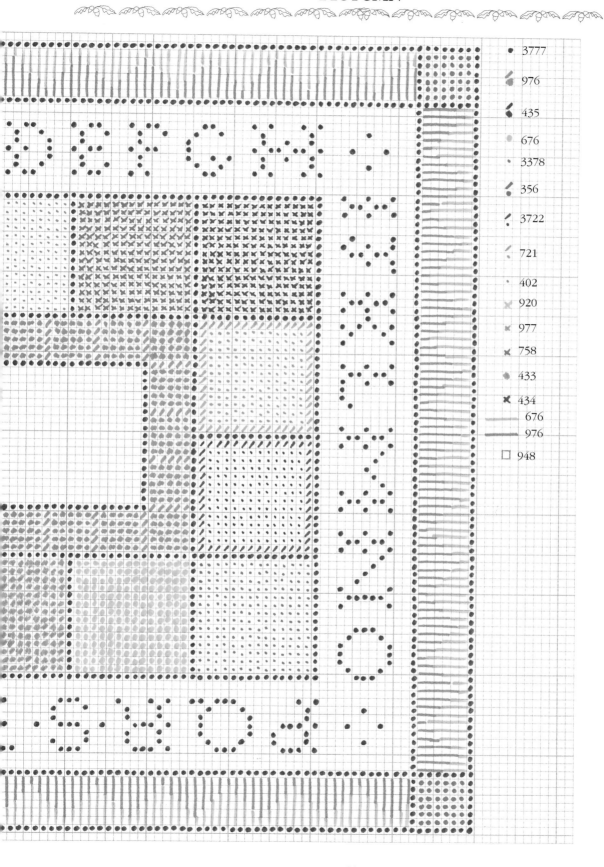

•	3777
	976
	435
	676
•	3378
	356
	3722
	721
•	402
✕	920
✕	977
✕	758
	433
✕	434
—	676
—	976
□	948

Lavender Sachet

The hazy blue of the Norfolk lavender fields creates one of the most beautiful sights of the countryside. Dried lavender flowers are perfect for perfuming this needlepoint sachet

DESIGN SIZE 2⅛ x 2¾ in (5.5 x 7 cm)
STITCHES Tent stitch

□ Needle, size 22
□ Canvas 18 holes per inch (7 holes per centimetre), 5 x 5in (12.5 x 12.5cm)
□ Stranded cottons (floss) as listed on chart key. Use three strands of thread unless stated otherwise in the instructions
□ Backing fabric (cotton), 5 x 5in (12.5 x 12.5cm)

□ Kapok
□ Sachet of dried lavender
□ Blue ribbon, ⅛in (3mm) x 6in (15cm)

DMC	COLOUR	ANCHOR
791	Dark blue	178
792	Blue	177
809	Pale blue	130
3782	Beige	388
Blanc	White	01

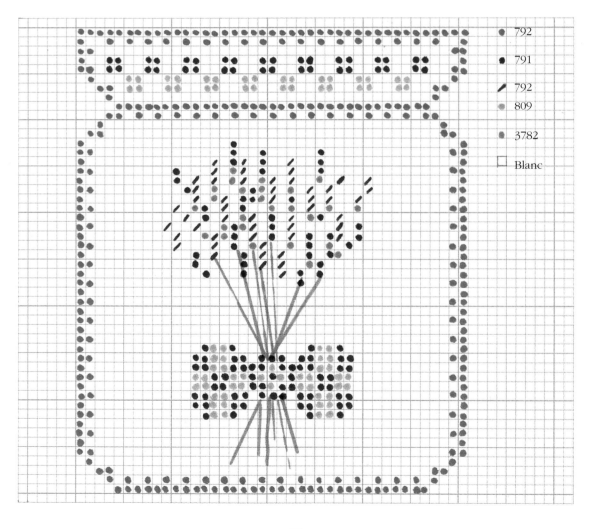

792
791
792
809
3782
Blanc

1 Find and mark the centre point on the canvas (see page 9).

2 Count from the centre point to the top right-hand corner of the border and start stitching here. Work colour by colour leaving the white background until last.

3 Using two strands of beige thread, oversew the stalks.

4 Block your needlepoint (see page 17).

5 Complete the sachet by following the instructions in steps 4 and 5 of the Tartan Scissor Weight on page 106.

6 Fill with Kapok and the lavender sachet before sewing up the fourth side.

7 Stitch the ribbon in place on the top left-hand side.

Lavender Sachet and Aster Anniversary Card (page 92)

Aster Anniversary Card

The vibrant colours of the Aster brighten up the autumn garden and here make delicate posies surrounding the initials. For special anniversaries work the initials in silver or gold

DESIGN SIZE 3 x 2in (7.6 x 5cm)
STITCHES Tent stitch, basketweave stitch, flower stitch, French knots, chain stitch

☐ Needle, size 22
☐ Canvas 18 holes per inch (7 holes per centimetre), 6 x 5in (15 x 12.5cm)
☐ Stranded cottons (floss) as listed on chart key. Use three strands of thread unless stated otherwise in the instructions
☐ Card mount, three-fold with pre-cut 3 x 2in (7.6 x 5cm) oval aperture

1 Find and mark the centre point on the canvas (see page 9).
2 Using the chart on page 125, and the instructions on page 17, work your chosen initials.

3 Work the plain blue background in basketweave. Stitch the flower heads in flower stitch placing a French knot in the centre of each completed flower. Using two strands of green, oversew the stems. Using two strands of green, stitch the leaves in chain stitch.
4 Block your needlepoint (see page 17).
5 Make up the card by following the instructions on page 17.

DMC	COLOUR	ANCHOR
800	Pale blue	120
603	Pink	57
3609	Lilac	96
793	Blue	176
742	Gold	303
989	Green	215

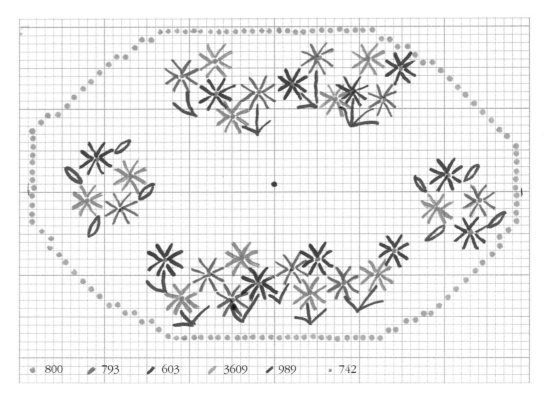

● 800　　╱ 793　　╱ 603　　╱ 3609　　╱ 989　　• 742

Blackberries Tile

It is always a wonderful sight to see the early autumn hedgerows, turning to copper and bronze, heavy with the ripening fruit of the blackberry

DESIGN SIZE 3⅝ x 3¾ in (9.3 x 9.5cm)
STITCHES Tent stitch, basketweave stitch, backstitch

☐ Needle, size 22
☐ Canvas 18 holes per inch (7 holes per centimetre), 6½ x 6½ in (16 x 16cm)
☐ Stranded cottons (floss) as listed on chart key. Use three strands of thread.

1 Find and mark the centre point on the canvas (see page 9).
2 Count from the centre point to the top right-hand corner of the border and start stitching here. Work the border colour by colour.
3 Fill in the fruit details, then the background in basketweave.

4 Block your needlepoint (see page 17).
5 Mount and frame as preferred. This picture was professionally mounted and framed using a lacquered wooden frame.

DMC	COLOUR	ANCHOR
3345	Dark green	269
3347	Green	261
772	Light green	259
3346	Mid green	262
349	Red	13
744	Yellow	301
436	Brown	375
939	Very dark blue	127
327	Blackberry	873
3042	Pale blackberry	870
Blanc	White	01

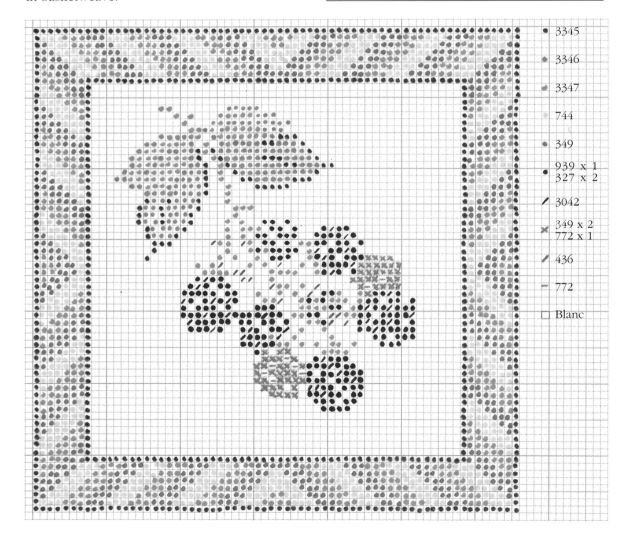

•	3345
♦	3346
▮	3347
•	744
•	349
•	939 x 1 / 327 x 2
╱	3042
✕	349 x 2 / 772 x 1
╱	436
−	772
☐	Blanc

Autumn Garden Picture

Gathered apples lie in wicker baskets on the long grass of the orchard,
succulent blackberries entwine themselves along the fence – a golden
view of the autumn garden

746	✖ 349	● 3347	● 680	· 3045	✖ 550 x 1 3685 x 2	● 610
━ 676 x 2 729 x 1	╱ 610 x 1 3781 x 2	3347 x 2 3013 x 1	· 3013	╱ 3011	● 3362	
▢ Blanc	╱ 3011	745	✖ 3363	· 800	╱ 676	━ 610

DESIGN SIZE 2⅞ x 4in (7.3 x 10 3cm)
STITCHES Tent stitch, cross stitch, brick stitch, basketweave stitch, French knots

☐ Needle, size 22
☐ Canvas 18 holes per inch (7 holes per centimetre) 6 x 7in (15 x 17cm)
☐ Stranded cottons (floss) as listed on chart key. Use three strands of thread unless stated otherwise

1 Find and mark the centre point on the canvas (see page 9).
2 Count from the centre point to the top right-hand corner of the wicker fence and start stitching here.
3 Work the trees in tent stitch and then go over with French knots. Using one strand of brown, oversew the bramble branches. Work the leaves in chain stitch.
4 Work the borders and the diamond outlines of the side panel in perlé. Fill in the panel following the chart, in tent stitch.
5 Block your needlepoint (see page 17).

6 You can mount this picture together with the Spring, Summer, and Winter Garden scenes in one frame as shown on page 2.

DMC	COLOUR	ANCHOR	STITCH
3011	Green	845	Tent
3362	Leaf green	861	French knots
3363	Leaf green	860	French knots
3347	Green	843	Tent
3013	Pale green	842	Tent
610	Brown	889	Tent
			Cross (trunks)
3781	Dark brown	0905	Tent
676	Corn	891	Tent
			Brick (path)
729	Dark corn	890	Brick
745	Pale yellow	300	Tent
349	Red	13	Cross
680	Dark beige	901	Cross
3045	Beige	943	Cross
800	Sky blue	120	Basket
Blanc	White	01	Tent
550	Dark purple	102	French knots
3685	Wine	70	French knots
746	Cream Perlé 5	300	Tent

You may add the title 'Autumn' (charted below) to the top or bottom of this design

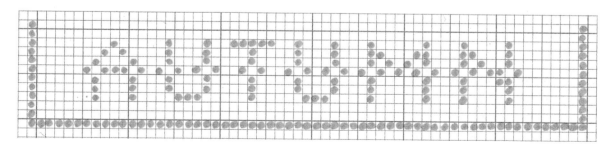

WINTER

I leant upon a coppice gate
When Frost was spectre-gray,
And Winter's dregs made desolate
The weakening eye of day.
The tangled bine–stems scored the sky
Like strings of broken lyres,
And all mankind that haunted nigh
Had sought their household fires

THOMAS HARDY

Winter – crisp, frosty days, with rimed trees sparkling in the watery sun. During the early weeks, Christmas is very much on our minds, an ideal time to stitch a card or gift for an appreciative friend. Metallic threads and coloured beads are wonderful for adding extra glitter. Why not brighten up your home with a sparkly hand-stitched Christmas decoration? When all the festivities are over, relax by picking up a piece of needlework – the rich and warm colours of the cranberries winter tile make a perfect project.

Christmas Stocking Decoration

This jolly Christmas stocking makes a lovely tree decoration. Fill with old-fashioned sweets – barley sugar, a candy walking stick, sugared almonds – or a special, tiny gift.

DESIGN SIZE 2¾ x 3½ in (7 x 8.9cm)
STITCHES Tent stitch, double cross stitch

☐ Needle, size 22
☐ Canvas 18 holes per inch (7 holes per centimetre), 6 x 6in (15 x 15cm)
☐ Stranded cottons (floss) and metallic threads

as listed on the chart key. Use three strands of thread unless stated otherwise
☐ Backing fabric (cotton), three pieces, 6 x 6in (15 x 15cm) each
☐ Metallic gold cord ⅛in (3mm) thick, 6in (15mm) long

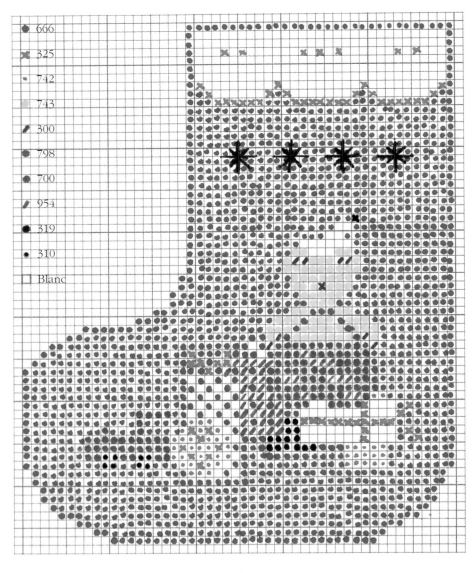

●	666
✕	325
●	742
▨	743
◢	300
●	798
●	700
◢	954
●	319
●	310
☐	Blanc

DMC	COLOUR	ANCHOR
666	Red	46
319	Dark green	212
742	Gold	303
700	Green	228
954	Light green	203
798	Blue	131
300	Brown	371
310	Black	403
743	Yellow	302
Blanc	White	01
Madeira	Metallic Gold	325

Christmas Stocking Decoration and Jewelled Moon Decoration (page 102)

1 Find and mark the centre point on the canvas (see page 9).

2 Count from the centre point to the top of the teddy's head and start stitching here. Work colour by colour, leaving the metallic gold and the background until last.

3 Stitch the teddy's nose and the bobble on his hat with a single cross stitch. Using one strand of black, stitch a French knot to create his eyes. Stitch the row of dark green double cross stitches.

4 Block your needlepoint (see page 17).

5 With right sides of the backing fabric and needlepoint facing, pin in place.

6 Backstitch around the stocking as close to the needlepoint stitches as possible. Leave a 2½in (6cm) opening on the right hand side.

7 Trim the canvas and fabric to ¼in (5mm) from the edge of the stitching and cut across the corners and into the curves.

8 Turn inside out and ease out the corners. Press gently from the back with a steam iron.

9 Repeat steps 5 to 8 with the two pieces of backing fabric.

10 Now, with the wrong sides together, very neatly stitch the two stockings together leaving the top open and closing up the two sides

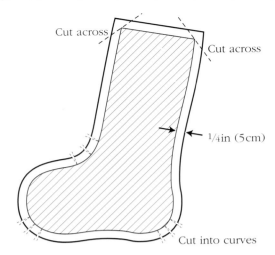

Making up the stocking

previously left open for turnings. To hang the stocking up, make a loop using 6in (15cm) of metallic gold cord.

Jewelled Moon Decoration

Sprinkled with metallic stars and jewel-like beads, this crescent moon will add a little extra sparkle to your Christmas decorations

DESIGN SIZE 5 x 5in (12.7 x 12.7cm)
STITCHES Tent stitch, diagonal mosaic stitch

□ Needle, size 22
□ Beading needle
□ Canvas 18 holes per inch (7 holes per centimetre), 8 x 8in (20 x 20cm)
□ Stranded cottons (floss) and metallic threads as listed on the chart key. Use three strands of thread unless stated otherwise in the instructions
□ Tiny glass seed beads in red, green and clear
□ Backing fabric (cotton), 8in (20cm) square
□ Kapok
□ Ribbon, ⅛in x 8in (3mm x 20cm)

1 Find and mark the centre point on the canvas (see page 9).

2 Count from the centre point to the left-hand border. Tent stitch the border, and then stitch all the stars.

3 Work the background in diagonal mosaic stitch.

4 Block your needlepoint (see the instructions given on page 17).

5 Using one strand of yellow, sew on the coloured glass beads.

6 With the right sides of the backing fabric and the needlepoint facing, pin in place including the ribbon.

7 Backstitch round the edge of the moon as close to the needlepoint stitches as possible, leaving an opening 2½in (60mm) on the left-hand outside curve. Trim the canvas to ¼in

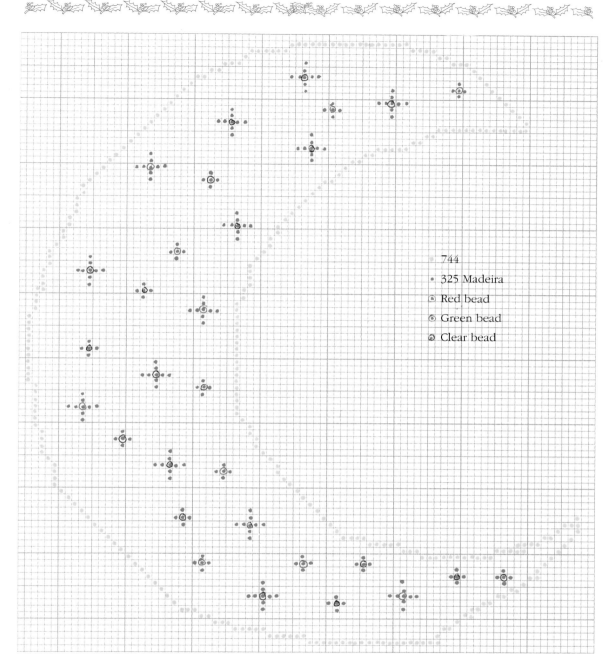

744
• 325 Madeira
⊙ Red bead
◉ Green bead
⊘ Clear bead

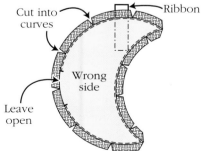

Making up the moon

DMC	COLOUR	ANCHOR
744	Yellow	301
Madeira	Metallic gold	325

(5mm) from the edge of the stitching and cut into the curves.

8 Turn inside out and ease out the corners. Press gently from the back with a steam iron. Fill with the kapok and stitch up the opening.

Tartan Needlecase

Tartan is now firmly associated with Christmas. A stunning mix of red and green, brightened with white and yellow, makes a particularly festive project

DESIGN SIZE 2¾ x 3½in (7 x 9cm)
STITCHES Cross stitch

- ☐ Needle, size 22
- ☐ Canvas 18 holes per inch (7 holes per centimetre), 6 x 6½in (15 x 17cm)
- ☐ Stranded cottons (floss) as listed on chart key. Use three strands of thread
- ☐ Backing fabric, 5 x 12½in (13 x 31cm) cut into two pieces: A – 5 x 8 1/2 in (13 x 21cm); and B – 5 x 4in (13 x 10cm)
- ☐ Wadding, ½in (1 cm) thick, 2¾ x 3½in (7 x 9cm)
- ☐ Cord, yellow, ¼in (3mm) x 40in (100cm)
- ☐ Felt, 3 x 4½in (8 x 12cm)

DMC	COLOUR	ANCHOR.
Blanc	White	01
743	Dark yellow	305
666	Red	46
321	Dark red	47
700	Green	228

1 Find and mark the centre point on the canvas (see page 9).

2 Count from the centre point to the top right-hand square and start stitching here. Work the white last.

3 Block your needlepoint (see page 17).

4 Place the finished needlepoint right sides together with backing fabric B.

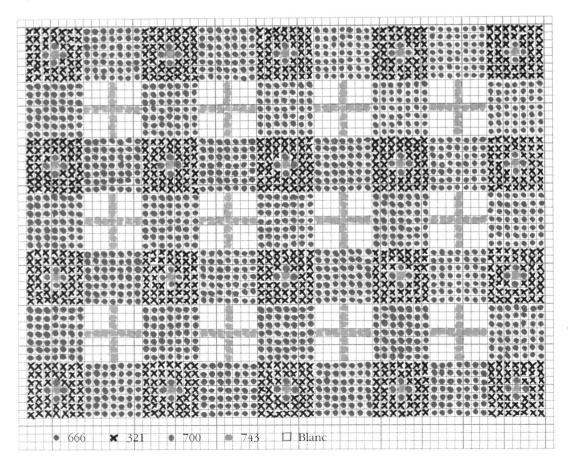

| • 666 | ✗ 321 | • 700 | • 743 | ☐ Blanc |

Tartan Needlecase and Tartan Scissor Weight (page 106)

5 Stitch along one long side as close to the cross stitches as possible. Press out seam and trim to ½ in (1 cm) from the edge of the stitching.

6 Place this piece right sides together with backing piece A. Stitch around three sides, leaving the short side where the backing fabrics meet open. Trim to ½ in (1cm) from the edge of

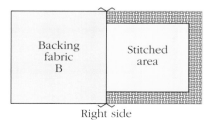

Joining the needlepoint to backing fabric B

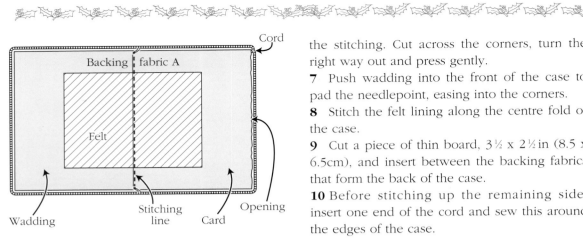

Making up the needlecase

the stitching. Cut across the corners, turn the right way out and press gently.

7 Push wadding into the front of the case to pad the needlepoint, easing into the corners.

8 Stitch the felt lining along the centre fold of the case.

9 Cut a piece of thin board, 3½ x 2½ in (8.5 x 6.5cm), and insert between the backing fabrics that form the back of the case.

10 Before stitching up the remaining side, insert one end of the cord and sew this around the edges of the case.

Tartan Scissor Weight

This bright tartan scissor weight matches the pretty needlecase on pages 104 and 105, and together they make lovely Christmas gifts, acceptable additions to any sewing box

DESIGN SIZE 2½ x 2½ in (6.5 x 6.5cm)
STITCHES Tent stitch, basketweave stitch

☐ Needle, size 22
☐ Canvas 18 holes per inch (7 holes per centimetre), 6 x 6in (15 x 15cm)
☐ Stranded cottons (floss) as listed on chart key. Use three strands of thread
☐ Backing fabric (felt, cotton or silk), 4 x 4in (10 x 10cm)
☐ Kapok or sheep's wool to stuff
☐ Cord, yellow, ¼ in (3mm) x 15in (40cm)
☐ Ribbon, yellow, ⅜ in (1cm) x 30in (75cm)

1 Find and mark the centre point on the canvas (see page 9).

2 Count from the centre point to the top right-hand corner and start stitching here. Use basketweave stitch for the solid red and dark red squares. Use tent stitch for the yellow and white squares.

3 Block your needlepoint (see page 17).

4 Put right sides together with the backing fabric and stitch around three sides using back-

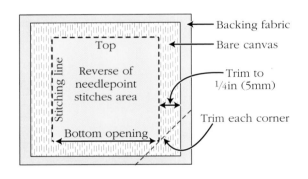

Making up the pincushion

stitch and as close to the needlepoint stitches as possible.

5 Trim edges to ¼ in (5mm) and cut across corners diagonally. Turn inside out and ease out the corners. Press with a steam iron from the reverse.

6 Fill with padding. Before sewing up the fourth side, insert one end of cord and attach.

7 Sew cord to edge of scissor weight, and insert second end before sewing up the remaining gap (see diagram opposite).

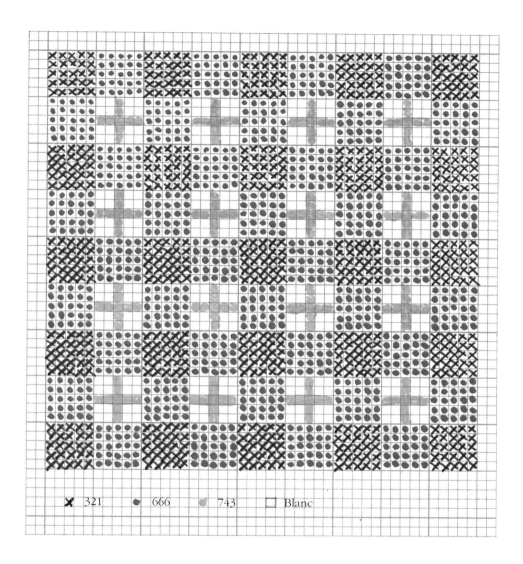

| ✗ | 321 | ● | 666 | ● | 743 | ☐ | Blanc |

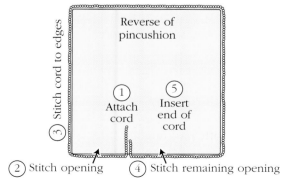

Adding the cord

DMC	COLOUR	ANCHOR
666	Red	46
321	Dark red	67
Blanc	White	01
743	Dark yellow	305

8 Fold ribbon in half and sew the ends to the back of the scissor weight where the ends of the cord meet. Tie a small bow in the remaining ribbon and stitch onto the front of the scissor weight, also where the cord ends meet.

Star and Moon Hair Bow and Buttons

*Gleaming moons and sparkling stars put you in the festive spotlight.
This glittering hair bow and matching buttons transform any Christmas
or party outfit*

DESIGN SIZE Bow 2¾ x 5in (7 x 12.5cm);
Button 1¼ in (3.3cm) diameter
STITCHES Tent stitch, double cross stitch,
basketweave stitch

BOW

- □ Needle, size 22
- □ Canvas 18 holes per inch (7 holes per
  centimetre), 6 x 8in (15 x 20cm)
- □ Stranded cottons (floss) and metallic thread as
  listed on chart key. Use three strands unless
  stated otherwise

- □ Backing fabric (Chinese silk dupion), 6 x 8in
  (15 x 20cm)
- □ Wadding (batting), ½in (1 cm) thick
  2½ x 4¾in (6.6 x 12cm)
- □ Barette hair clip, 3in (75mm) long

DMC	COLOUR	ANCHOR
823	Blue	127
333	Purple	119
DMC	Gold fin or Mi fin 5g	
Madeira	Metallic gold	325

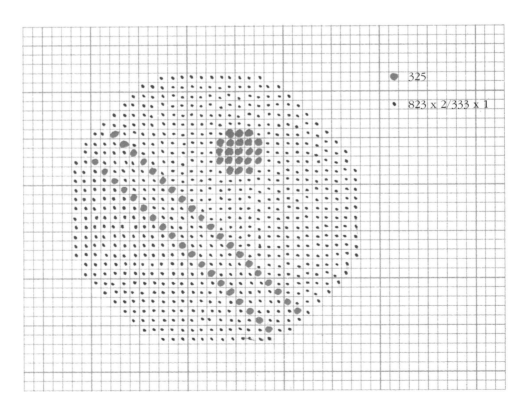

● 325

• 823 x 2/333 x 1

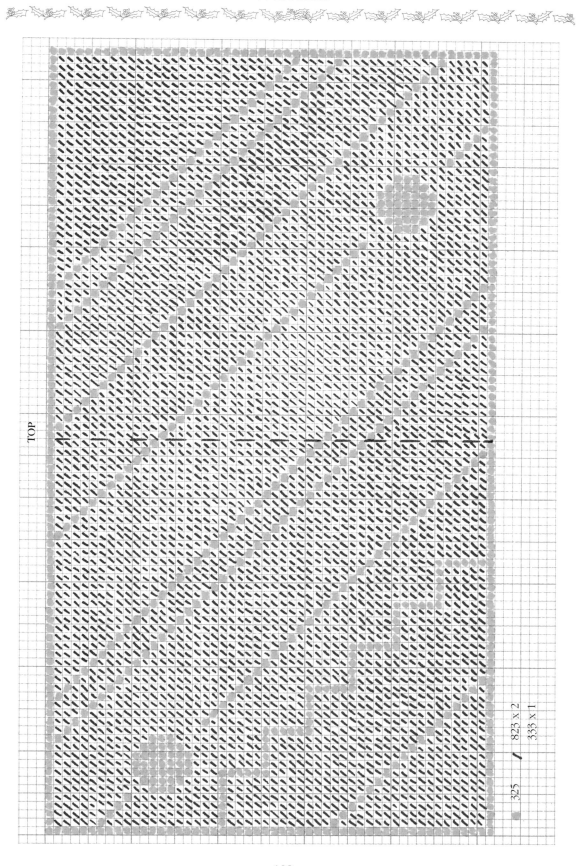

TOP

325

823 x 2
333 x 1

1 Find and mark the centre point on the canvas (see page 9).

2 Count from the centre point to the top right-hand corner and, using the gold metallic thread, work the outside border and the moons in tent stitch.

3 Work the remaining metallic thread in tent stitch and then fill the background using basketweave stitch.

4 Using one strand of fine metallic gold thread, work double cross stitches randomly between the diagonal lines.

5 Block your needlepoint (see page 17).

6 Make up into a bow (see page 57).

BUTTONS

□ Canvas 18 holes per inch (7 holes per centimetre), 4 x 4in (10 x 10cm) per button

□ Metal buttons size 3, – 1⅛ in (2.9cm)

1 Work the gold metallic thread first in tent stitch, then the background in basketweave stitch. Using one strand of fine metallic thread, finish the design by adding glittering random double cross stitches.

2 Follow metal button maker's intructions for clamping button canvas into place. Make up into buttons by following the instructions given on page 59.

Jewellery Pouch

Worked mainly in Florentine stitch, this soft pouch will hold precious pieces of jewellery. It looks equally striking in other colourways

DESIGN SIZE 5¾ x 3in (14.5 x 7.6 cm)

STITCHES Tent stitch, florentine stitch

□ Needle, size 22

□ Canvas 18 holes per inch (7 holes per centimetre), 8¾ x 6in (22 cm x 15cm)

□ Stranded cottons (floss) and metallic threads as listed on chart key. Use three strands of thread

□ Glazed cotton backing fabric, 18 x 8 in (50 x 20 cm)

□ Metal button, ¾ in (19mm)

□ Sewing thread

1 Find and mark the centre point on the canvas (see page 9).

2 Count from the centre point to the top right-hand edge of the border, and stitch the border. Fill in with florentine stitch, then oversew with the metallic thread.

3 Stitch the button design.

Opposite Star and Moon Hair Bow and Buttons and Jewellery Pouch

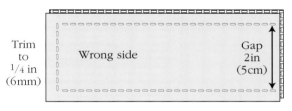

Stitch round edge of needlepoint

Backing the embroidery

4 Block your needlepoint (see page 17).

5 Cut a piece of the backing fabric to 8¾ x 6in (22 x 15cm). Place the needlepoint and the backing fabric right sides together. Using a suitably coloured thread, backstitch around the needlepoint as close to the edge of the border as possible. Leave a gap of 2in (5cm) open on one of the short sides. Trim the canvas to ¼ in (5mm) from the edge of the stitching. Turn the right way out and press gently.

6 Cut two pieces of backing fabric 6¾ x 6½ in (17 x 16.6cm). With right sides together,

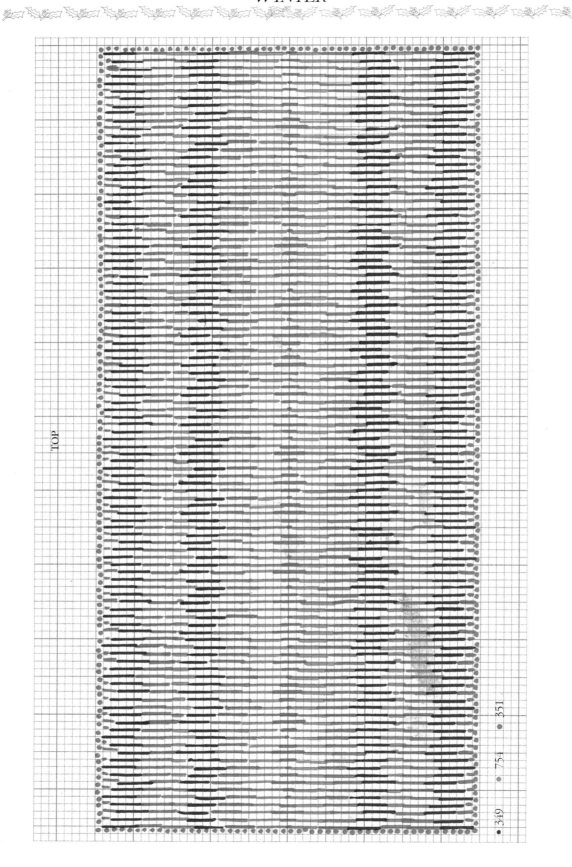

TOP

• 349   • 754   • 351

DMC	COLOUR	ANCHOR
349	Dark peach	13
351	Peach	10
754	Pale peach	6
Kreinik Balger Fine Braid 8		Red 003

backstitch all round ½in (10mm) from the edge, leaving a 2½in (6.4cm) gap. Trim to ¼in (5mm) from the edge of the stitching, turn the right way out and press gently, easing out the corners.

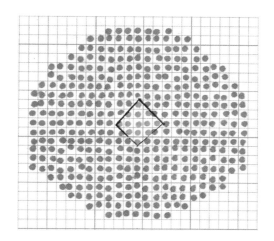

Jewellery pouch button chart

Tuck in the remaining raw edges of material and sew up neatly.

7 Place the needlework and the backing square together and hem stitch along the top edge. Fold up the backing fabric to make a pouch and stitch up the two short sides.

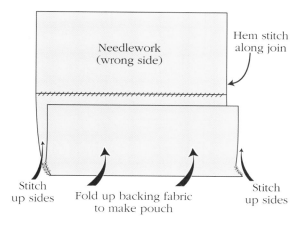

Making up the pouch

8 Follow metal button maker's instructions for clamping button canvas into place. Stitch centrally onto the bottom edge of pouch.

9 Create a loop for the button using some metallic thread.

Christmas Parcel Card

Glittering presents with a border reminiscent of holly leaves – all the richness of Christmas is contained within this sparkling little card

DESIGN SIZE 2½ x 2½in (6.5 x 6.5cm)
STITCHES Cushion stitch, diagonal mosaic stitch, tent stitch, sloping gobelin stitch, long stitch

□ Needle, size 22
□ Canvas 18 holes per inch (7 holes per centimetre), 6 x 6in (15 x 15cm)
□ Stranded cottons (floss) and metallic threads as listed on key. Use four strands of thread
□ Gold foil card mount, three-fold with pre-cut 2½ x 2½in (6.5 x 6.5cm) aperture

1 Find and mark the centre point on the canvas (see page 9).
2 Count from the centre point to the large blue parcel on the chart. Find this point on your fabric and start stitching here.
3 Work the red inner and outer borders in sloping gobelin stitch. Then fill in between with the rope pattern.
4 Block your needlepoint (see the instructions given on page 16).
5 Make up the card by following the instructions on page 17.

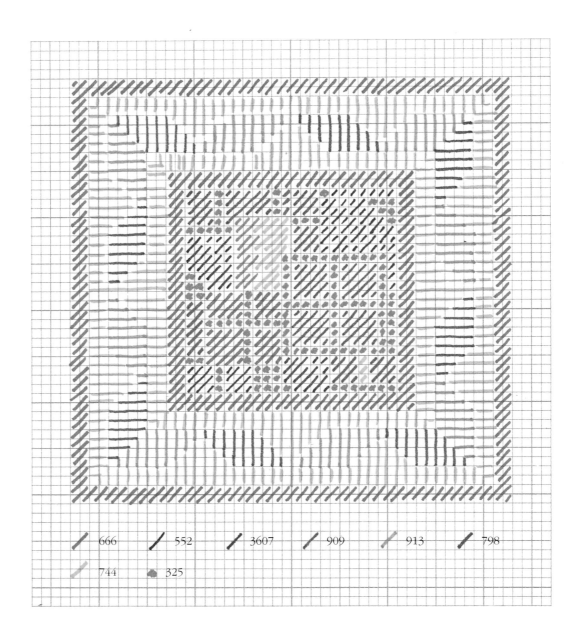

DMC	COLOUR	ANCHOR	STITCH
666	Red	46	Sloping gobelin (borders)
			Cushion (parcels)
744	Yellow	305	Long (borders)
			Satin (parcels)
913	Light green	204	Long (borders)

DMC	COLOUR	ANCHOR	STITCH
909	Green	230	Long (borders)
			Cushion (parcels)
798	Blue	137	Cushion (parcels)
552	Purple	101	Diagonal
3607	Pink	87	Diagonal mosaic Cushion
Madeira	Metallic gold	325	Tent

Criss Cross Scotties Card

These cute little Scottie dogs on a brightly checked background make an unusual Christmas greeting, or a jolly card for a December birthday

DESIGN SIZE 2½ x 2½ in (6.4 x 6.4cm)
STITCHES Tent stitch

□ Needle, size 22
□ Canvas 18 holes per inch (7 holes per centimetre), 4½ x 4½ in (11.5 x 11.5cm)
□ Stranded cottons (floss) and metallic threads as listed on the chart key. Use three strands of thread unless stated otherwise in the instructions
□ Green card mount, three-fold with 2½ in (6.4cm) pre-cut square aperture.

1 Find and mark the centre point on the canvas (see page 9).

2 Count the number of stitches from the centre point to the top of the centre dog's ear and, using four strands of black, start stitching here. Work colour by colour, leaving the metallic threads and background until last.
3 Block your needlepoint (see page 17).
4 Make up the card by following the instructions on page 17.

DMC	COLOUR	ANCHOR
666	Red	46
700	Green	228
798	Blue	131
310	Black	403
742	Gold	303
Madeira	Metallic gold	325

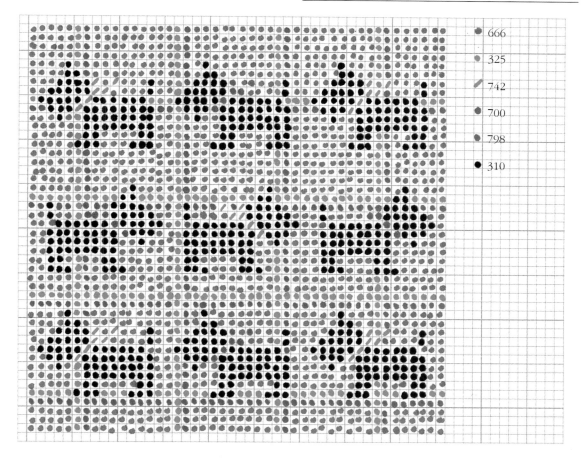

- 666
- 325
- 742
- 700
- 798
- 310

Valentine Patchwork Picture

Inspired by American folk art, this miniature patchwork of hearts can be mounted as a special Valentine's Day card, or framed to become a lasting treasure

DESIGN SIZE 3⅛ x 3⅛in (9 x 9cm)
STITCHES Tent stitch, basketweave stitch, cross stitch, running stitch

- Needle, size 22
- Canvas 18 holes per inch (7 holes per centimetre), 8 x 8in (20 x 20cm)
- Stranded cottons (floss) as listed on chart key. Use three strands of thread unless stated otherwise in the instructions
- Handmade paper, 5½ x 11in (14 x 28cm)
- PVA glue

DMC	COLOUR	ANCHOR	STITCHES
3722	Dark pink	1026	Tent (large hearts) Cross (small hearts)
3712	Mid pink	895	Cross
760	Salmon pink	1023	Tent (large hearts) Cross (small hearts)
224	Pink	894	Tent (large hearts) Cross (small hearts)
225	Pale pink	1021	Tent (large hearts) Cross (small hearts)
730	Green	844	Cross
948	Pale fawn	892	Basketweave

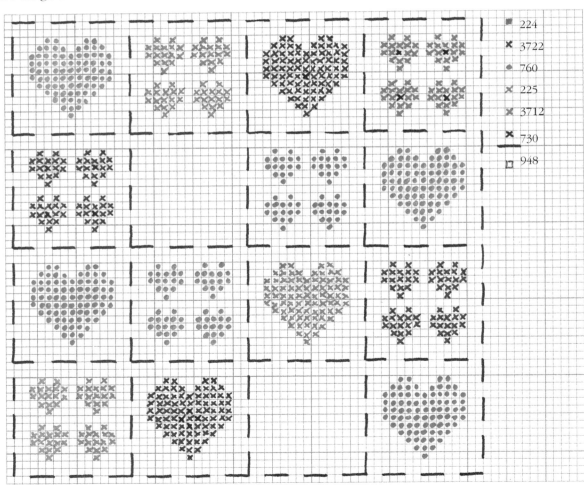

■	224
✕	3722
●	760
✕	225
✕	3712
✕	730
▢	948

Winter

1 Find and mark the centre point on the canvas (see page 9).

2 Count from the centre point to the top right-hand group of hearts and start stitching here. Work all the hearts. Using one strand of dark pink, outline the very pale pink small hearts in backstitch. Using one strand of green, outline the very pale pink large heart in backstitch.

3 Using the alphabet on below, and following the instructions on page 16, stitch your initials into the empty squares in mid pink.

4 Work the background in basketweave stitch. Then use green and a running stitch to divide the patchwork squares.

5 Block your needlepoint (see page 17).

6 Remove the canvas threads on all four sides, one at a time, to create a fringe.

7 Fold the paper in half to make a card and attach the patchwork to the front with glue. Alternatively, see page 17 for advice on mounting and framing.

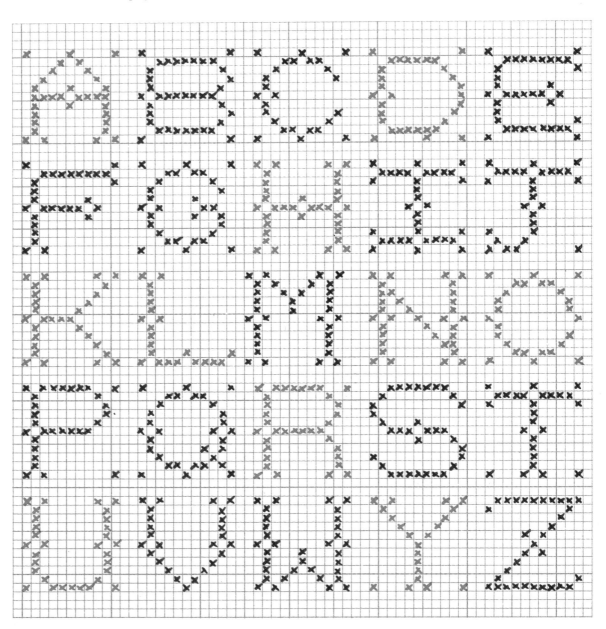

Snowy Sheep Picture

A little winter scene of sheep in the snow (pictured on pages 98–99), ideal as a mini picture for yourself or a friend, or as an alternative Christmas card

DESIGN SIZE 2½ x 2½ in (6.4 x 6.4cm)
STITCHES Tent stitch, cross stitch

☐ Needle, size 22
☐ Canvas 18 holes per inch (7 holes per centimetre), 4½ x 4½ in (11.5 x 11.5cm)
☐ Stranded cottons (floss) as listed on chart key
☐ Use three strands of thread

1 Find and mark the centre point on the canvas (see page 9).
2. Count the number of stitches from the centre point to the bottom horizontal line of the fence and start stitching here.
3 Build up the picture by sewing the sheep

and tree before filling in the background details. Stitch each sheep's head as one single cross stitch. Leave the snow flakes until last.
4 Block your needlepoint (see page 17).
5 Mount and frame as preferred. Our picture was professionally mounted and framed.

DMC	COLOUR	ANCHOR
794	Blue	939
700	Green	228
300	Brown	371
666	Red	46
319	Dark green	212
310	Black	403
3031	Dark brown	380
Blanc	White	01

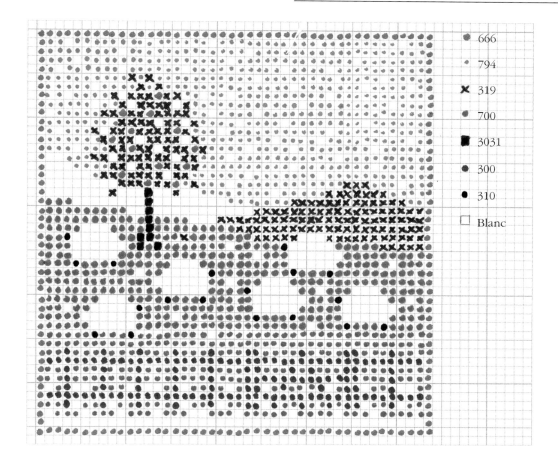

●	666
•	794
✖	319
●	700
■	3031
●	300
●	310
☐	Blanc

Cranberries Tile

*A cluster of jewel-like berries will bring a little
cheer on the darkest of winter days,
and make a bright and colourful centre
to this framed miniature*

DESIGN SIZE 3⅝ x 3¾ in (9.3 x 9.5cm)
STITCHES Tent stitch, basketweave stitch, backstitch, French knots

□ Needle, size 22
□ Canvas 18 holes per inch (7 holes per centimetre), 6½ x 6½ in (16 x 16cm)
□ Stranded cottons (floss) as listed on chart key. Use three strands of thread unless stated otherwise in the instructions

1 Find and mark the centre point on the canvas (see page 9).
2 Count from the centre point to the top right-hand corner of the border and start stitching here. Work the border colour by colour.

3 Fill in the fruit details, then the background with basketweave. Stitch the French knots.
4 Block your needlepoint (see page 17).
5 Mount and frame as preferred. This picture was professionally mounted and framed using a lacquered wooden frame.

DMC	COLOUR	ANCHOR
742	Yellow	302
814	Burgundy	43
326	Cranberry	1025
3347	Green	266
3345	Dark green	268
471	Light green	255
746	Cream	386
3346	Mid green	267
Blanc	White	01

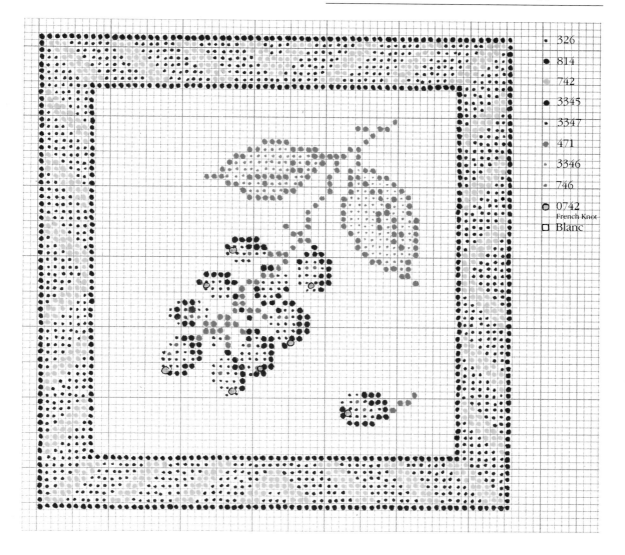

•	326
●	814
●	742
●	3345
•	3347
●	471
•	3346
•	746
○	0742 French Knot
□	Blanc

Winter Garden Picture

An old stone sundial sits amidst the snow in this corner of the garden. The freezing white of deepest winter is broken only by the splash of bright red holly berries

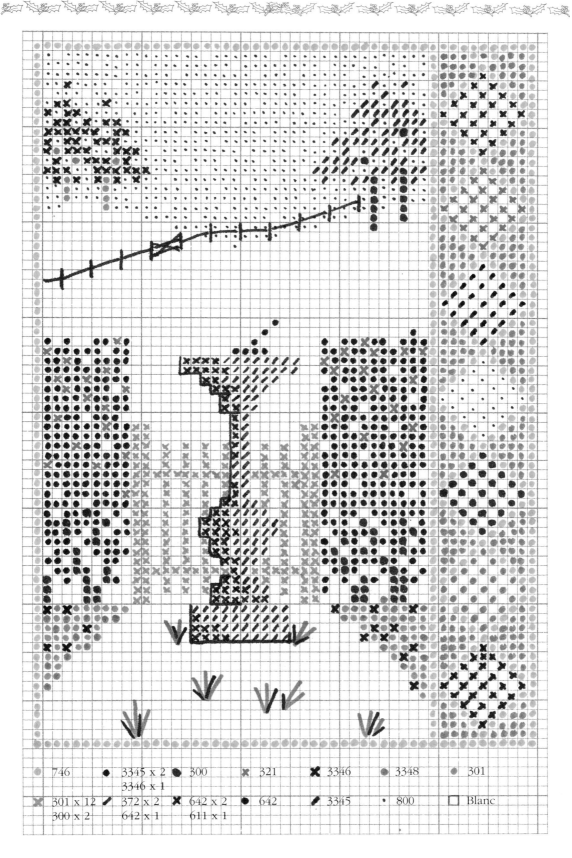

	746	●	3345 x 2	●	300	✕	321	✖	3346	●	3348	●	301
			3346 x 1										
✖	301 x 12	╱	372 x 2	✖	642 x 2	●	642	╱	3345	·	800	☐	Blanc
	300 x 2		642 x 1		611 x 1								

DESIGN SIZE 2⅞ x 4in (7.3 x 10.3cm)
STITCHES Tent stitch, cross stitch, French knots, basketweave

□ Needle, size 22
□ Canvas 18 holes per inch (7 holes per centimetre), 6 x 7in (15 x 17cm)
□ Stranded cottons (floss) as listed on chart key. Use three strands of thread unless stated otherwise

1 Find and mark the centre point on the canvas (see page 9).
2 Count from the centre point to the sundial and start stitching here.
3 Using one strand of dark green, outline the sundial in backstitch where shown. Next, using one strand of mid green and one strand of light green, oversew the blades of grass. Then, using one strand of grey, oversew the distant fence in the background.
4 Work the borders and the diamond outlines

of the side panel in perlé. Fill in the panel in tent stitch.
5 Block your needlepoint (see page 17).
6 You can mount this picture together with the Spring, Summer and Autumn Garden scenes in one frame as shown on page 2.

DMC	COLOUR	ANCHOR	STITCH
Blanc	White	01	Basketweave
800	Sky Blue	120	Basketweave
3345	Dark green	263	Tent
3346	Mid green	262	Tent
			French knots (leaves)
3348	Light green	264	French knots
300	Brown	371	Tent
301	Light brown	309	Tent
321	Dark red	47	Cross
611	Dark grey	903	Cross
642	Grey	392	Cross
			Tent (sundial)
372	Olive green	945	Cross
745	Cream perlé 5	300	Tent

You may add the title 'Winter' (charted below) to the top or bottom of this design

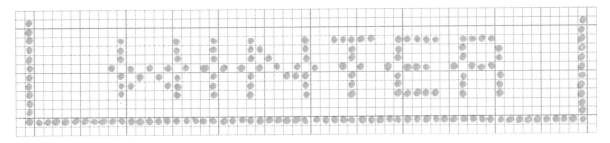

Alphabets

Mothers Day Card and Brooch (pages 25 and 27)
and Aster Anniversary Card (page 92)

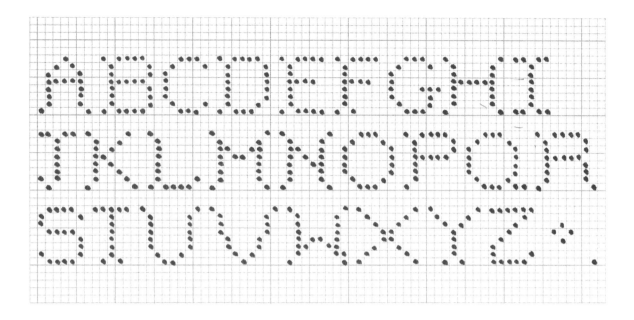

Patchwork Cushion Number Chart (page 86)

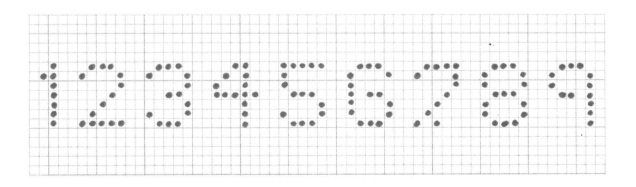

Alphabets

Wedding frame (page 60)
Tooth Fairy Pillow (page 22)

Suppliers

THREADS AND CANVAS

DMC Creative World Ltd
Pullman Rd, Wigston, Leicestershire, LE18 2DY
Tel 0116 281 1040   Fax 0116 281 3592

U.S.A.
DMC Corporation
10 Port Kearny, South Kearny, New Jersey
07032, U.S.A.
Tel 201 589 0606

Coats Crafts UK (for Anchor threads)
PO Box 22, The Lingfield Estate, McMullen Rd,
Darlington, Co. Durham, DL1 1YQ
Tel 01325 394 394 Fax 01325 394 200

U.S.A.
Coats & Clark
PO Box 24998, Greenville, South Carolina
29616 - 24498, U.S.A.
Tel 001 864878 5546

De Havilland Embroidery (for English flower
threads)
Monomarch House, Old Gloucester St, London
WC1 3XX

Madeira Threads UK Ltd (for metallic threads)
Thirks Industrial Park, York Rd, Thirsk, North
Yorkshire, Y07 3BX
Tel 01845 524 880 Fax 01845 525 046

FRAMES, BOXES AND BEADS

Framecraft Miniatures Ltd
372-376 Summers Lane, Hockley, Birmingham
B19 3QA
Tel 0121 212 0551 Fax 0121 212 0552

GREETINGS CARD BLANKS

Craft Creations
Unit 1-7 Harpers Yard, Ruskin Rd, Tottenham,
London N17 8QA
Tel 0181 885 2655 Fax 0181 808 0746

NEEDLEPOINT KITS

Thumbelina Designs
10 Barley Mow Passage, Chiswick, London W4
Tel 0181 994 6477

Acknowledgements

We would like to thank our friends and family for all their support
and encouragement whilst we have been compiling this book. We
would also like to thank the team at David & Charles especially
Cheryl, Jane and Kay for their professional advice and assistance,
and Di Lewis for her wonderful photography.

Index